Quest of Soul

Esoteric Teachings of the Tradition of Tao

BOOK TWO

Quest of Soul

By Taoist Master
NI, HUA-CHING

The Shrine of the Eternal Breath of Tao
College of Tao and Traditional Chinese Healing
LOS ANGELES

Acknowledgement: Thanks and appreciation to
Janet DeCourtney and Frank Gibson and the students
of the Center for Taoist Arts for assistance in
typing, proofreading and editing this book.

The Shrine of the Eternal Breath of Tao, Malibu, California 90265
College of Tao and Traditional Chinese Healing, 117 Stonehaven Way
Los Angeles, California 90049

Dedicated to those who know the wise way
to fulfill one's spiritual responsibility
is to nurture one's own spirit and
to join the universal soul.

To female readers,

According to Taoist teaching, male and female are equally important in the natural sphere. This is seen in the diagram of Tai Chi. Thus, discrimination is not practiced in our tradition. All my work is dedicated to both genders of human people.

Wherever possible, constructions using masculine pronouns to represent both sexes are avoided; where they occur, we ask your tolerance and spiritual understanding. We hope that you will take the essence of my teaching and overlook the superficiality of language. Gender discrimination is inherent in English; ancient Chinese pronouns do not have differences of gender. I wish for all of your achievement above the level of language or gender.

Thank you, H. C. Ni

Warning - Disclaimer

This book is intended to present information and techniques that have been in use throughout the orient for many years. The information offered is to the author's best knowledge and experience and is to be used by the reader(s) at their own discretion. The information and practices utilize a natural system within the mind and body, however, there are no claims for their effectiveness. It is not a cure-all like the claims of conventional religions.

Because of the condensed nature of the information contained within this book, it is recommended that the reader of this book also study the author's other books for further knowledge about a healthy lifestyle and energy conducting exercises.

The author and publisher of this book are not responsible in any manner whatsoever for any harm which may occur by misapplication of the instructions in this book.

CONTENTS

Prelude

"Tao is the destination of all religions, while it leaves behind all religions just like the clothing of different seasons and different places. Tao is the goal of serious science, but it leaves behind all sciences as a partial and temporal description of the Integral Truth.

"The teaching of Tao includes all religious subjects, yet it is not on the same level as religions. Its breadth and depth go far beyond the limits of religion. The teaching of Tao serves people's lives like religions do, yet it transcends all religions and contains the essence of all religions.

"The teaching of Tao is not like any of the sciences. It is above the level of any single subject of science.

"The teaching of Tao is the master teaching of all. However, it does not mean the teaching relies on a master. It means the teaching of Tao is like a master key which can unlock all doors leading to the Integral Truth. It teaches or shows the truth directly. It does not stay on the emotional surface of life or remain at the level of thought or belief. Neither does it stay on the intellectual level of life, maintaining skepticism and searching endlessly. The teaching of Tao presents the core of the subtle truth and helps you to reach it yourself."

Preface

There are three kinds of people who will be interested in reading this book. The first kind of people have some religious background and they just kind of go along with it. They were taught about the importance of having a soul and saving the soul and so forth. However, they have never experienced such a truth as was taught to them. Perhaps some partial experience was attained by the initial spiritual leaders of their religion, but those leaders were never able to prove or show their complete knowledge, even if they had it. Even in the teaching of mysticism, they are still unable to present the truth. Thus, such spiritual establishment has become no more than a kind of make-believe. It does not have a matter-of-fact attitude.

The second kind of people do not accept the conventional, make-believe and religious thoughts. They are suspicious about spiritual reality. Although they feel that a person must have a soul, just as fruit has seeds, they are not satisfied and cannot accept the old type of religious teaching. They are also without a way to establish any kind of objective research to prove such a thing. Through many years and during many generations, some people may have tried to prove the existence of religious teaching without definite success.

The third kind of people are totally upset by the conventionally assertive religious teaching, and so they totally turn away from imposing religious thought. It is because the conventional religions try to take authority over people's souls or command over others, that the third type of people turn away from that control. After experiencing the unprovable teaching of general religions, they learned from the assertive religious way and simply decided that human life has no soul.

Those three kinds of people face one same reality. No one has real experience or can scientifically reveal the matter of the soul as a concrete fact for them. There is no one who can give them accurate information that they can accept, and who can help them understand the right attitudes to hold regarding their own soul.

In this book, I take advantage of the teachings of the ancient developed ones of the Taoist tradition. With their knowledge and experience, you may receive a new opportunity to solve the big question you have had for a long time. This book is not related to any conventional religious dogma. It does not suggest that, "I have to save you; you have to follow me. Otherwise, you will lose your soul." That is not the Taoist type of teaching.

If you have skepticism about your soul, I will give a practice to help prove it for yourself. No one else shall build authority over your life. Also, I objectively and truthfully answer questions related to the subject according to what I have reached. After discovering the soul, you may know the right way to live, and the way to live with your own soul and to nurture your soul.

This is a short text among my works. The beginning chapters are a discussion between myself and some of my students. I offer you a correct understanding to start doing the practice which will prepare you to reach the step of knowing your deep self. At last, I give the important practice by which a person can discover that he has a soul. The reality of the soul is not just our imagination.

It is interesting to see that people in general live in the same house with their soul. It is the reality that the mind and soul exist in cohabitation. But they do not know each other. It is like they both live in the same apartment building and they come in and go out through the same door, but never know each other. The ancient achieved description is that they use the same six doors, but they do not know each other. This means that your soul and your mind both use the same two ears, two eyes and two nostrils. They mentioned six instead of seven because the soul energy does not usually go out through your mouth; it is the tongue which is moved by your mind. The mind also functions through the ears, eyes and nostrils. It receives the gathering of the senses and how they were stimulated to have various impressions; an important network of external communication has been built to receive messages and respond correctly. So although the same doors are used, the two neighbors within the being of most people have not yet become friends.

Sometimes people have a double-visioned mind. When there is harmony, the vision is one, but when there is conflict internally, then distorted images and inaccurate information is given. The establishment of modern psychology is based on fragmental facts about the mind and soul. No whole picture of human life has been seen by this young science. My attitudes and my kind of teaching recommend learning the natural truth.

This is one of my important works which fulfills my mission of spiritual awakening for all individuals. The human world has certainly come now to the stage where people need to know more. This is not the same as the time when our ancestors probed in the dark, step by step, to learn the truth.

So the three kinds of people I have mentioned, whether they are those who grant there is a soul, those who think there is no soul, or those who wonder if there is a soul, all of them will certainly be attracted to reading this book. It is hard to put a proper title on this book that will speak to all three kinds of people, so I called it *Quest of Soul.* It means I would like it to remain as a quest.

One meal cannot sustain a person's whole life. This is why I have a number of important books in English that work in different areas. If you have a chance, I wish you would consider reading them, because they are all related to the same subject, the natural spiritual reality of humans. Then you shall have the complete picture and not just enjoy a partial view. I hope you have all good new experiences by reading my books or doing the practices.

Ni, Hua-Ching
March 28, 1990

Chapter 1

The Teaching of the Unspoiled Soul

A talk given to a disappointed soul

First I would like to review a very old and at the same time very new subject. It is life. Life is not limited to the surface; it has a soul. In this moment, let us not talk about life, but about living. Living includes what is internal as well as what is external. For example, living people have emotions. Emotion is a reaction of the soul, at least in a lower level. In a conventional lifestyle, people resort to religion to help them with their emotions. It is a way to smooth or soothe the internal being, especially the lower sphere of bodily spirits. This is similar universally.

In the West, Christianity is the popular religion. In the East, three religions are most active: Hinduism, Islam and Buddhism. I was born in China, and at the time I was born, Buddhism was a popular religion in the Chinese region, Japan, Korea and other countries of Asia. Everything that exists under Heaven must have a reason for its existence. There must be a reason for the popularity, wide acceptance, and existence of a big religion. These religions were popular because of what they did to calm people's emotions when times were rough.

Today we have a chance to review our emotional life and to see or learn how we respond emotionally, or healthily, to matters that are of importance to us. It was around 2,500 or 2,600 years ago that Sakyamuni, or Buddha, was born into the Nepal tribe. The Nepal tribe was more closely related to the Chinese in custom and background than it was to the people who now live in India. Sakyamuni was a sage born into this small country in the south of the Himalayas. His blood connection, however, was with the people who live in the north of the Himalayas. Yet culturally, the greatest influence was from the south of India, where Hinduism was exalted. Jainism was also a cultural influence in India at that time. Jainism is a dualistic, ascetic religion founded in the 6th century B. C. by a Hindu reformer as a revolt against the caste system and the vague world spirit of Hinduism. All these cultural influences caused Sakyamuni to be enthusiastic in his spiritual pursuit. Through spiritual pursuit, he wished to find the answer and solution to a particular matter: life. From his wisdom, he clearly knew why the people in the south so warmly worshipped Brahma and so many other interesting deities: it was to obtain blessings. Those southern people truly believed that life is a blessing that comes from God.

This young man, a great philosopher with great potential in the stage of youth, experienced the special type of glory and comfortable life that comes with living in a luxurious palace. Sakyamuni was born the son of a royal family and was sheltered from experiencing the hardships of the world during his youth. Then he came to observe the life of ordinary people. This changed his religious attitude. Through his spiritual learning, he came to understand that it is not the worship of God that truly brings blessing to people. It is that people bless themselves and curse themselves. One's own spiritual attainment becomes one's own light and sees that life itself has nothing to do with the general religious approach or point of view.

Sakyamuni sat quietly under the Bodhi tree, and it came to his mind that life is composed of four things: the bitterness of birth, the bitterness of being old, the bitterness of being sick and the bitterness of dying. In birth, it is the bitterness of mother and child when the child is born into a life composed mostly of bitterness, emptiness and meaninglessness. Sakyamuni witnessed that after birth people grow old. All their hard work does not maintain them in freshness and good vitality, but the process of growing old continues. There is occasional sickness, which cannot be avoided totally by anybody. And finally, the life that was born with bitterness and lack of meaning, now returns with all the experience of bitterness, back to the meaningless void. He saw it. He knew it. All matters affected him emotionally. Therefore, he was looking for a way to overcome the experience of the bitterness of life.

After much searching, he finally discovered the peaceful mind. Maintaining peace of mind is the highest achievement, is the highest religion at that stage of a spiritual person's life. God is not a person who either bestows blessings upon you or decides that your destiny will be miserable. Each person's destiny is open to bitterness or freshness, depending on the choice of the individual.

His religion slowly developed in this way: how do we know there is bitterness? Because we have consciousness. How do we have consciousness? Through the senses. Then how do we know that the information we gather through the senses is truthful, is reality? If life is meaningless, then how do we know that the information we gather through our senses has any meaning? The denial of the value of life became the basic emotional structure of that religion.

In China many people who are in trouble, especially if they have been defeated by life, simply become Buddhist. Many people with emotional sensitivity escape to the worship of Buddha. You must understand that Buddha started as the philosopher Sakyamuni, but finally, in later times, people's imaginations transformed him into the image of a spiritual giant that could cure the bad emotion caused by the bitterness of their lives. This image of Sakyamuni as a spiritual savior was not his own creation. That image was not accomplished by him, nor was it a solution he recommended.

There are two levels of people who follow Buddhism: One level trusts Buddha as a great spiritual giant, as a God who can absorb all one's bitterness. The second level, when a person chooses to learn it, is the search for peace of mind, mixed up with the superstition of the existence of an external spiritual giant, like the worldly mind creates in all religious practice.

I use the elements and thoughts about this story to review how Sakyamuni's earnest teachings were twisted to make him look like a spiritual savior. I do not envy him, because there is no true spiritual achievement in this.

Buddhism does offer a spiritual escape and has helped people throughout generations, for at least a thousand years in China. Men and women with strong emotional problems have been helped by finding escape or refuge there. The extreme ones shave their heads and wear gray to become nuns and monks.

The teaching and religion of Buddhism would express the difference between Christianity and Buddhism. Christianity is the promotion of a faith that grasps the mind of the believer. Underneath, in the mind of the believer, lies the same bitterness of emotion that cannot be faced, so the believer finds a conceptual spiritual giant which can absorb all his problems. Suffering emotional disappointment, people bend and twist their natural life being, whether it is a healthy being or a sick being, to receive the emotional consolation of following a religion.

Can we define the bitterness of life or the bitterness of birth? The natural viewpoint of life is not to see bitterness. The natural viewpoint is that through universal spiritual nature, all life is brought about. All life rides on the universal creative energy; thus, we are born. No woman who has cried from the pain of birth will be discouraged, because the joy of the new life she has brought into the world is much greater than the pain she suffered. A baby is an invisible natural energy that has come through the mother's womb into a small human body. It has a chance to gather new elements, and when the time is ripe, it finally shapes himself or herself as an adult human with great potential for future progress and continual spiritual evolution. The process is the same whether it is a baby boy or a baby girl. Once born into the world, when the first mouthful of fresh air on earth is breathed, the life is established. It is new progress; the natural energy from the low sphere and from the invisible sphere hold the tremendous promise of the future.

I do not know if it can be established, as religions point out, that there is a sense of bitterness at the moment the mother gives birth to the baby. It was the courage of the mother and the courage of the young spirit that brought together the continuation of the life of the universe. All mothers are goddesses and all babies are gods. Through the worldly experience, the sense of self slowly becomes stronger and stronger. Not long after, the happiness of winning and the bitterness of losing is felt. There is an important lesson for this new life to achieve: it is how to be a good winner and a good loser. In life, sometimes you need to give something up and sometimes you need to take something. On both occasions, the bitterness or joyfulness that you experience depends on you, the young god or goddess, and how you accept the outcome.

At one stage, the state of all lives was natural. I do not know how anyone could objectively define the process of life as bitterness at that time. It was not until the establishment of an unnatural society that bitterness could have been established. When there is a ruler and the ruled, the person in the high position suppresses the slaves. This type of division formed the old pattern of life within the last 3,000 years.

Once the human world became overly organized, naturalness was broken. Human beings lived in nature for many years before the undeveloped mind started to dominate the sphere of human life. The mind began to dominate only about 3,000 years ago, but humans existed much longer than that. That earlier period was a time of naturalness.

At the beginning, the teaching of religion was different. It was a warning for people to give up their competition, ambition, aggression, greed and hatred, so they could take a better step forward. Those negative attributes are not part of man's original nature. They are picked up from the worldly life experience. Living with those things brings one to think that the world is hell and there must be someplace else which is heaven. It is only people who hold such an attitude that make it so.

When people talk about the bitterness of life, it is because they are afraid of death. Their fear expands and absorbs all parts of their lives. From that fear, they begin to deceive or cheat others. After discovering they have made a mess of their lives, they look to religions for help. But the religions can only offer emotional support. All the people really wanted in the first place was to join in the natural dignity of the spirit of natural life. That is their true nature.

So friend, you need first to find your naturalness. Do not talk about bitterness. Bitterness is not your nature. It is a psychological composition which you create with your life experience. I wish you would learn objectivity. With objectivity, a person can look at his life to review the emotional elements. After that review, he can come back to look for spiritual completeness. In that way, a person can become a good student of life. We call such a person a student of Tao, the truth of wholeness.

If a person goes the other way, he remains a student of death, a student of the worldly death religions. Which way will you go? In this moment, I can show you the opportunity for the recovery of your natural being.

Many people invest their time, emotion and energy to live. Some objective people discover that each individual has a destiny. Among all flowers, some blossom in spring and some blossom in autumn. Some give seeds and fruit, but some do not give flower or seeds at all. Similarly, each individual has natural traits. Unfortunately, society generally promotes wealth, high position, good times, beautiful marriage and many obedient children as blessings or as the only good things in life for every person. Some people truly enjoy these things, some are dismayed by them, and others think about them. Not all of those things are beneficial for all people.

Yet, people work hard to attain the standard of general society because they think that it is what other people achieve and enjoy. They lose their own inner understanding of what is beneficial for them. They do not understand that each individual has his or her natural trait. You cannot use one standard to evaluate a rose and a chrysanthemum. You cannot use one standard to measure or value the worth of different lives.

However, all cultures, Eastern and Western, have developed ways to prophesize a person's destiny. The different systems can, more or less, tell what will be brought about or experienced by an individual. Because the measurements used by these systems are still money, position, marriage, children, friends, and so forth, some will be happy about their so-called good fortune. Others, however, find their happiness does not lie in comparing themselves to others but in accepting whatever their fortune is. They are like a duck with short legs that does not bother to compare itself to the egret, who has long legs. Each individual has its own standard, which is best understood when not looking at others. There is no external, singular measurement that decides the value of a life. I discovered, in my development as a spiritual person, that so-called fortune or destiny is still external and therefore does not have the greatest value in a person's life. Why is it not of the highest value? Although it can be foretold or described as good or bad, it is always associated with external experience. One's true destiny is internal, and true destiny cannot be told.

Seeing the many different kinds of personal destiny that are possible brought people to want to understand the reasons for the differences. So the theory of karma was developed. The theory of karma brings forth the reincarnation of soul. The theory of recyclable soul brings forth the liberation from karma and the deliverance of the soul. The theory of liberation from karma brings forth the ascetic way of life. The theory of deliverance of the soul brings forth the God of Justice and the Goddess of Mercy. You see how the human mind begins with something and then continues to add to it. All the theories are a kind of unnatural development. Spiritually, they create a mess.

Many people are bothered by their destinies, though external destiny is only an objective gathering of such information as whether a person can be married, can have good children or can become rich. They do not see that all the different traits of life, seen and unseen, are valuable and respectable. They only regard the old culturally promoted standards and then measure themselves.

Astrology is a useful tool in some way. Because I learned at least three or four different systems in Chinese astrology, I am well versed in it. When I use those methods, I can almost always find out accurately what has happened in an individual's life. The external life experience depends so mechanically on how an individual responds to each situation.

What is more interesting is that people are born with strong or weak spiritual tendency and interest. People who allow the one-sided guidance of practical life to dominate do not find truth. The balance of life is the most valuable principle.

I would like to take a little time to talk about good fortune and bad fortune. In Chinese astrology and Western astrology, life is divided practically into twelve aspects of individual fortune, with cyclic changes. We can use this structure to talk about the twelve aspects of life: birth, family, parents, siblings, marriage, personal achievement, helpers, money and finance, travel, health, emotional condition and residence. These twelve aspects combine together to decide one's fortune.

Simplified, there are two basic types of life situations: either good or bad, favorable or unfavorable. However, most good life situations are not noticeable. Only the bad ones are experienced by people; they sting a person to make him awake and aware of the problem that has occurred. What most people also do not notice is that the greatest spiritual development comes from the so-called bad occasions, not from the smooth, unnoticeable hours or days. So, good times are the days that slip away unnoticed, and bad times are the days that teach you something. You develop yourself from facing the bad times. This is called using each situation to your own benefit.

It is the hard times that bring about the meaning of life. Facing - not running away from - the trouble and success one receives will bring future spiritual achievement. Who welcomes bad times? But yet, bad times make such a big contribution in life. It is important for people of spiritual development to keep their mind poised to support their soul in good times in order to prepare or strengthen the spiritual ability to stay poised in bad times. In this new study, all people focus on the search for their own unspoiled soul, which encompasses the common soul of nature and of the whole human world. Then, all can come together in improving the world, in creating a paradise of soul and body for everyone with awareness of the inseparable well-being of the spiritual world and the physical world.

Q: I have been aware of, and consciously following Tao, since probably June or July of 19xx. However, in retrospect, my lifestyle differences and path have been a partial and dim understanding. Actually, all of my life has been following Tao, but finding no one of like beliefs or energy, has caused me to veer from my path little by little until 1989.

Since meeting Master Ni in Seattle last summer and beginning to read his books, I am experiencing rapid and over-whelming changes in my life, my body and my spirit. It is almost like flipping the pages of a book - I myself am changing that much.

Now, I have two problems of concern. One: I am a widow for nine years. I have no other relationship and do not look for one. My husband was part xxxxxx of a Shaman line, and four months before he died at age 38 of a heart attack, he wrote an invocation binding me to him for all time. I burned the invocation years ago to release myself. His ghost or spirit (I do not quite understand which) has remained around where his son, xxxxx, and I are, although I do not acknowledge or speak to it. Psychics see him here - I sense him. On one occasion, he saved xxxxx's life.

A year ago, a man from New York read an article that I wrote for a dance magazine and wrote to me. My husband appeared to him at night and spoke to him.

After my husband had been dead for around two months, he came to me and asked me to follow him. That time I did speak to him and told him to go.

Last summer I could feel him very strongly. I stepped outdoors and my neighbors cried, "Look! Look! Over your head!" There was a male and female red tailed hawk (his Indian symbol - and in the invocation he spoke of us as being red tailed hawks forever). The hawks were circling over my head, the male swooping lower.

Two nights ago, our son xxxxx had a nightmare, which came after 2 or 3 days of over-concern about my safety. In this dream his dad appeared and was quite aggressive, and tried to force him out of the house saying that my husband wanted to take me with him.

xxxxx is also following Tao and said, "Mom, I cannot tell if the contact was with my dad or some other spirit, but the presence was intense."

This morning, I could strongly feel my husband's presence.

I only want spiritual freedom and independence, and a chance to achieve myself. I am reading the invocation from the Workbook for Spiritual Development of All People, *cultivating every day.* I use the tai chi symbol over my bed and my truck, but this presence is quite foreboding and intense right now. I need to know how to keep myself and my spirit safe from harm from this ghost or whatever it is.

My son said, "Mom - you meet a lot worse than this. You must work to cultivate yourself. Be sincere and keep your heart pure and the integral realm will help you." But how do I deal with the spirit?

My second problem is that in my line of work I deal with people who are very ill. I am an exercise physiologist and I also sell xxxxxxxx herbs. All of a sudden, since January, people have been "sent" to me that, because of troubles inside of them, I would avoid if I could. For example, a woman of 345 pounds with a bowel blockage, full of dark, strange, black energy, a 410 pound man, a woman with breast cancer metastasized to her bones. I gently guide these people to change their lives. I do not deal with the spirits within them. Master Ni said not to visit the sick, but I cannot avoid it because it is my line of work. I am aware of the energies and spirits. How can I protect myself? I know that I have been challenged by some of these spirits. I feel like a naive child. I simply read "The Highest Divinity of Universal Response" ten times and do the four characters for "There is peace under Heaven," in addition to reading invocations, doing the meditation of the five clouds, and the thirty-six swallows of energy every morning. Sometimes if I know that I will be dealing with someone like the cancer patient, I try to step into my bedroom and read a few invocations before I leave to see them.

The more I cultivate, the more I know that these things are troubling the people. Sometimes I see strange things in their bodies.

Please help me understand how to protect myself.
If I were developed would I perhaps not be troubled by
this? I am embarrassed that I do not know what to do.

Master Ni: This response is to the question about the past
husband that is haunting you. There are a number of
things that a person can do. The first thing, please remember one thing. An alive person has a power to summon
spiritual beings, so firstly you need to thoroughly clear the
mind. It means that any time you think of the person, the
ghost appears. So never think about *something or someone*, if it is not a welcome thought. How you do stop thinking about someone? I would say, in the house and surroundings, anything belonging to the past, belonging to the
person or that the person used can become a reminder to
your thoughts and make a suggestion of who had used it.
Then through your thoughts, you summon the ghost. So
the trouble is you; it is not the ghost. So the first thing is
to avoid the memories and thoughts of the passed person.
If you cannot do that, then know it is you that asks him to
come rather than he who likes to do it. This is because you
always command with your alive energy. Alive energy is
much stronger with natural energy. It is stronger than the
ghost of a deceased person.

The second thing is to never emotionally reject it. If
you reject something emotionally, the emotion means internal struggling. That makes the trouble stronger. It makes
the image of the ghost stronger because it is how you empower the ghost. The ghost itself has no power.

So maybe these are the two mistakes that you are
making in your life. The first would be, by good thoughts
or bad thoughts, always to think of the passed husband.
But even when the thoughts are not welcome thoughts, but
you keep thinking them. The second mistake is emotional
rejection that causes the attachment to be stronger.

The thing to do to solve your problem connects with
the mind. The mind has a power. If your mind is not correct, then any exorcism would work only a little bit, not
very much.

My practical suggestion is that you move to a new place, and make new friends to be new. Touch nothing in the past, but more importantly, renew your psychology, as a new person with a new life.

There is one bit of special knowledge I need to tell you. Sometimes it is not the ghost. All ghosts, if not achieved, usually lose their freedom in the underworld. Although nobody knows if there is a government or not in the underworld, the ghost is not as free as human beings. Any object is the product of the emotion of a person; because each person has his own spiritual energy, it always reflects your fears, hatred and whatever. Because your mind is strongly related with the person, then your spiritual mirror shows it like that and you mistake it as a ghost. Most ghost cases come from this type of situation.

Do you know how big a ghost is? A ghost is as small as the tiniest grain of sand. A ghost can never appear until it rides on your nervous system; then it appears as big as you are. So you build the ghost and you nurture the ghost. If you do not thoroughly achieve yourself, you might ruin yourself, by your own self and by any people surrounding you that have the memory of your husband. People do this; they make stories to feed each other poison.

I believe that since you have been married, he is not an enemy. A person can even talk with an enemy and can make peace. I do not think there is anything that cannot be dissolved. At least he was your husband, unless you murdered him. I cannot say anything, but he does not have the right to make a disturbance for you. It does not matter if he is doing shamanism or Buddhism or anything.

About your second problem, you need to build yourself stronger and learn the serious spiritual practice before you do anything. A person with no training cannot jump into the arena to look for the championship in boxing combat. This is a kind of special training. First of all, modern people do not believe it. Second of all, if they believe it, they do not usually make use of it. They hardly find the teacher or have the patience really to set up a schedule to do that. I believe that the best way to do this is to follow my instructions. First, do not think about the person; second, do not hate the person or even mention him; third, rectify your own mirror. That is all. It seems that you wish an answer could come as the exorcism type of activity. It is a different pursuit. Those who pursue such an unpopular and primitive skill start their training very young with a pure and fresh mind and spirit. In truth, there are lots of fake exorcisms. Nothing really works.

Everything is related to your mind. It seems that the practice of the mind is the effective way to eliminate your suspicion and fear. Otherwise you should stop all the higher practices because the progress of your positive sphere of life seems to intensify the negative sphere of life at the same time. Such a struggle shall have no end. It may be fatal, if you do this way and constantly keep suggesting this kind of emotional problem to yourself.

The cultivation you do is for people who have basic psychological health. If a person is a little weaker, it is alright to use the practices to build back one's health. To people who are impure psychologically - this means having some special bad experience - it is like a cancer patient who is taking in lots of nutrition that makes the cancer prosper rather than improving their general health condition. You need a diet. It means what is needed is stronger, useful spiritual discipline which can be found in the *The Key to Good Fortune: Refining Your Spirit (Heavenly Way)*, especially the section entitled, "Straighten Your Way" (Tai Shan Kan Yin Pien). This should be intensely worked out.

Righteousness is a reality of God, or reality of power. In the human world, physical strength might be used to create a temporary circumstance. In the spiritual world, a pound of righteousness is stronger than 10,000 tons of TNT. Your weakness is an internal conflict. Surely you can insist and think that it is a ghost problem, but if you insist, you are going to finish yourself. I call this spiritual transfer.

I mentioned at the beginning that one effective practice is to avoid the old energy. I have seen many Masters who achieve themselves spiritually with strong determination, not by avoiding but facing it, and viewing it as personal measurement of how much they have achieved in virtue and spirit.

The ghost problem is the fertilizer of the prosperity of general religions. For the need for emotional dependency, all big images were created; they support the internal weakness. You do not look at it. A real God is only going to be at the side of a righteous one. If you correct your virtuous condition, it is necessary to increase the power within you. God will come to your side and be your friend rather than the other, unvirtuous spirits.

Shamanism is one stage of human religion. Tibetan masters revised it to be Buddhism. The original Taoism is a much higher level than shaman practice, which assists the ungrowing mind and spirit to make people need to look for external protection or to help them to become rich or get a good marriage. It can be done by your own interest if your goal is limited to worldly interests. I will recommend such a thing as folk Taoism or a similar level of religions to you. Unfortunately, the hope for improvement and development will be continued through lifetimes of self-created pity.

The greatest and most powerful exorcism practice is to face the sun, face the moon and face the stars, face the ocean, face the mountain, etc. All of them constitute the picture of human life. There is no position for a ghost unless your mind becomes the mother of such a low birth.

My friends who work with me read my books. Their mind only grows to give birth in one lifetime to an angel which will replace the earthly life some day after their virtuous fulfillment.

To those who have spiritual ambition, it is not difficult to find a good teacher to help you achieve spiritually. It is difficult for a student to use the opportunity to correctly learn the example of the spirit of life and cultivation of the teacher. The teacher does his work not for a commercial purpose, but for a pure spiritual purpose. It should be avoided that the teacher-student relationship become a heavy emotional pull. If such a thing occurs, it would be more suitable for a student to be on a different level, such as a believer or follower of a religion, from which he or she would receive emotional support. That type of learning is fit for a level of emotional dependency rather than truthful spiritual learning.

In my case, most of my students are sensitive and supportive. This means that if they could not help in my spiritual work, at least they will not use their heavy emotion to force my attention away from my important work just to look at the mess of their monkey within.

Also, if a person wishes to learn and achieve immortality, it is not suitable to live on donations, sort of like the parasite type of religious custom. One needs to take care of one's own life and make preparations for one's concentrated spiritual practice. Unless there is extreme difficulty or if a person is too old, it is better not to build a habit of depending on the social welfare of society. If you are capable and powerful, you might become the one supporting the world. If all the time you attempt to turn the world to your favor to support you, it destroys the quality of spiritual purity.

More importantly, to learn from a teacher is to learn ⎞ the teacher's discipline and cultivation. Learning the virtue of the teacher does not mean to become a follower to keep flock with the teacher. That is a different level. It is also right to learn from the teacher's example of constantly working on himself and helping new people in a general level. Never use a spiritual teacher like a child looks to its mommy or daddy. In this type of relationship, a student would never receive any spiritual growth, and he would be wasting his time.

Some people use conventional religious attitudes towards a serious spiritual learning. It is a spiritual obstacle to the individual himself and would create a disturbance to the teachers' concentration of his own spiritual direction. Students in this level need to keep reading and learning from a general teacher who fits his or her stage and by group study. He or she has no need of personal contact with a teacher who teaches immortality. If that is what a person wants without first improving himself, he or she would not make much out of any opportunity of receiving special spiritual instruction from a teacher.

A tadpole will transform into a full size frog. It has its own internal possibility to do so if put in a natural environment. By this I mean, it is not the grace from any teacher that transforms a person. Do not believe that you need the teacher who can do the most for you. If you present a frog to a teacher and ask him to change it to be something else, and if the frog nature within the being has not changed, it is still a frog. True change comes from within oneself, not from an outside person.

This is the key point: each individual needs to work from inside to outside. External teachings may give people some light, especially as a spiritual confirmation or a mirror. A teacher's response serves as a mirror and helps a student know iin what stage he is and the goal and direction in which he needs to go. Different students receive different responses depending on their development; the help or lack of help they receive from the teacher varies depending on many factors.

In one word, it is the spiritual qualities within oneself that decides the achievement and the real being of what the person is. That is the only thing that counts in spiritual learning; not the attention of the teacher. The teacher has the same cultivation to do to refine his own spiritual reality. The spiritual world is fair and just. No compromise exists. To keep searching would delay your real spiritual benefit unless you start to work on the shortcomings of your own spiritual progress.

Chapter 2

An Individual Life Contains
The Truth of the Entire Universe

Thank you, my friends, for joining us this afternoon. I am really happy to see all of you. More important than your being here today is the fact that you are looking for a life with internal worth, something which is not measurable by numbers. Some of you are new; perhaps some of you recognize me to be your teacher, but you are here today looking for a direction for your spiritual growth.

When I use the words, "I" or "my," you can also substitute the words, "us" or "our," because what I have to say relates to all of us and not just to myself.

So I would like to read this for you. You may have some difficulty understanding my accent, but you will soon become used to it. You will not be mistreated by my language. However, the heart is more important than the mind and the mind is more important than the ear, in case you still cannot understand.

Remember, this message relates to you and all of us, not just to me. This message can give a direction or focus to anyone who is searching spiritually.

"The purpose of my life is to increase the good life of all people and all lives.

"The mission of my life is to continue the life of the universe.

"The direction of my life is to be the essence of all human life, to be the conscience of the world, to be the mind of universal nature, to continue the achievement of all ancient sages, and to be the point where all people of all future generations can harmonize with each other.

"For the above reasons, I live, I work, and I make all possible effort to remove all obstacles on my way to my goal."

That is a short statement, but it contains much of the essence of Taoist inner understanding of universal nature.

What is also important today, is that I would like to share
with you the next part of our gathering, which is a general
chatting. We can converse and talk with each other. Let us
find out what you would like to discuss. Even though I shall
have about one whole week to be around Atlanta and other
nearby places, it is still a limited time. So I hope that all of
you become relaxed so that we can enjoy each other, and talk
about anything you would like to know.

Let me first start by speaking about the condition of the
world. Some people have strong confidence in their life. Their
confidence may come from good health or a good mental
condition, but they may not now have any true or conscious
knowledge about the spiritual level of life, which certainly
exists. Those people may never or may not have any spiritual
interest. They might think, for example, that their physical
strength is everything. They may tend to be cruel or brutal;
on some specific occasion, they will react that way and will
become outrageous in handling personal or public affairs.
This is something that often happens among the majority.

Another direction of the majority is accepting a conventional religious faith. What most people call religion is
usually nothing more than an organized psychological
program. Such programs promote a big image, real or unreal,
legendary or fictitious. However, the user of the religion
comes to depend on what they promote. They become
dependent on a social group, a certain religious vocabulary
and a narrow way of behavior. Then they lose their adaptabil-
ity to the changing reality of life. Sometimes the believers, if
they are strongly affected by the programming, also come to
doubt the reality of life and the world, of personal growth, and
at the same time, they blindly give up whatever achievement
they have made in the rational level. Because there are so
many of these different psychological programs in the form of
various religious sects, community or social programs,
systems of belief, etc., fighting arises among them. Those
programs use spiritual worship to support their emotional
and their psychological life in a childish way. However, our
main concern is not what people believe; anything that
positively and flexibly helps the world can be beneficial and
encouraging. What we are concerned about is the problem

that arises when two different such groups come into contact with each other: because of the different wording of their adopted beliefs, they end up fighting. In the world today, There is fighting between Islam and Christianity, two different religions. There is fighting between Islam and Hinduism, and also there is fighting between the different sects or explanations of Christianity. So far, how much progress or how high an achievement have the majority of human people reached? Instead, they spend their time fighting. It is trouble. It is a condition of undevelopment.

Let us look at how to attain spiritual growth in a different way. This tradition of two million years of experience lives in an independent environment. It provides a natural cultural condition without giving any specific program. The people respect the truth that heaven, earth and human people are equal. This tradition also respects human people as the middle point where the spiritual sphere called heaven and the material sphere called earth meet each other. While continuing the effort of individual spiritual awakening and growth, it does not establish an external doctrine which represents that the purpose of life is to serve any one of the three.

In correct words, the purpose of life as promoted by this tradition is to serve the spiritual growth of each individual self and of all people from this earthly foundation. You do not need to wonder: the human position in the universe is the integration of two different energies, material and spiritual.

These are all questions worthy of answering. The definitions given by the various religions are so different. This tradition of ageless truth, however, is looking for internal spiritual growth instead of mythological satisfaction.

We have already faced two situations. One is that of the follower of a certain religion who really does not have a clear idea about spiritual reality. The other is the situation of the overly-intellectual person who denies any spiritual reality without having any slight true spiritual knowledge. Let us understand more about these two opposites in the world and how they differ from the teachings of the Tradition of Tao.

The religious people have not attained internal spiritual development. On the contrary, because of their lack of development, they learn the need of relying on external religions. You, however, are different. You are here today looking for truth, not a new layout of shallow religious promotion. The mythology of different religions is an energy expression. Tao is the high truth behind the religions. Different religions have different mythological images, statues, pictures and so forth. They motivate people to believe in those things. When a person has not attained spiritual growth, he might accept the untruthful doctrines, fictitious stories and figures to falsely and emotionally support him. Most religious believers do not learn what the pictures or stories are really about. That is, they do not learn the truth behind them; thus, they believe in a fantasy. In the tradition of Tao, there are some pictures; these pictures symbolize the essential energy of your own life, physically, mentally and spiritually.

The other side of the majority believe neither in religion nor in accurate spiritual truth. They have never experienced or attained any truth of spirit nor understood what their spiritual experiences were. Because they do not understand themselves, they cannot communicate harmoniously with others so they continue their fighting and conflict. The trouble is constant and unending.

Despite these two prevalent attitudes of the majority, there sometimes is a good political or social leader who can temporarily put all the elements of society and the different mentalities together harmoniously for a certain period of time. If such a period happens, usually it is because the leader and the people have already suffered a long time as a result of meaningless, rough or difficult contention. So, to escape the difficulty, for a short time people awaken and agree to let the political or social leader guide them into having a good time. But soon, the differences again emerge. The fighting or war comes again. This type of situation is repeated over and over in world history. This type of cyclic alternation will continue until each of us attains spiritual growth through learning Tao.

Knowing the truth is not our pride; it is our learning and achievement, our duty and reward. In the past twelve year's work, I have been teaching and writing, wishing to give all of you, my beloved friends, a foundation upon which to grow. This is for you to have a basis upon which to start your own growth and make your connection with the attainment of the ancient sages. Once the base is established, then we see what we can learn from them and what we can develop further. That is the intention of this tradition in this new age.

I believe all of you have read some of my books and participated in some different classes. All of those things I hope to be truly beneficial to your natural, healthy life. Though each one of you wishes for the possibility to attain high spiritual achievement, all of us still need to associate with and assist each other. Achievement does not mean isolation. Through association with your spiritual allies, you can fully enjoy your growth and your healthy, complete life.

Do you have any questions about your study or your everyday life? You are welcome to present your questions.

Q: How would a Taoist respond to global destruction, for example, the destruction of the Amazon forests?

Master Ni: This is one problem expressing the undevelopment of people. The Taoist achieved ones usually have two attitudes about undevelopment. One attitude is that on a practical level, one suffers from the mistakes and the wrongdoings of the majority. But at the same time, he holds the other attitude and does not shun the responsibility to educate the majority.

I would not advise you to keep worrying about it, for two reasons. One reason is that the troublemakers know they have made enough trouble. If they are not going to stop the trouble, they are going to eat bitter fruit. They will not receive any true benefit from anything by continuing their actions. So what I am saying is that the universal energy response will teach them what they need to know; we do not need to worry endlessly about it. The second reason not to worry is that the greatest help that you can give to the world is to awaken yourself. Your own self development, with the help of the achieved spirits, will give the greatest influence to the world to change. A wish to promote goodwill is not enough; self-development is the key to accomplishing positive change in the world. Have you seen that the signs of hostility from the other side of the world are lessening? The country of jealousy used to say, "I am going to bury you, America." Now they do not say that anymore. Instead, the leaders came together to talk, saying "Let us slow down the arms race."

The world may find a way to live peacefully with all its elements in harmony. Who works on it? The high spiritual sphere. In general, people's image of spirits is that they must be monsters to be feared. They think this because they have experienced so much roughness in life. But spirits are not that way; it is only that the people themselves have not learned how to break off their imagination. Spirits are the essence of the universe. They are so tiny you cannot see them, but they are gentle, subtle and powerful. They can communicate with you if you are open enough; they can enter anytime into your brain to talk to you and make you understand things better. They will choose the right time to make all the ambitious leaders open their eyes to see what is the best solution for the improvement of the relationship of the human world. Because of this I know we need not worry about the big direction of where the world is going to move.

As an individual, instead of worrying, we might consider two important things: First, "Am I achieved enough?" We, as Taoists, work on ourselves because we need to prepare ourselves spiritually. If there is any big destruction or calamity, we will survive spiritually. That is why we get together and work hard.

The second thing to consider is to ask oneself, "Did I do enough to communicate with my friends about my new spiritual learning?" But be careful in your communication not to be aggressive. People cannot be forced to understand. People only learn when it is the right time for them to do so. All of you are here, waiting to receive higher awakening through your evaluation of what is said and presented today. You have high self-awareness that makes you able to do so. About your friends and your family, you can only occasionally, in the right circumstance, talk to them.

I do not know if this satisfies your question or not. My conclusion to this kind of problem is that people are authorized by their own spiritual nature, as individuals and whole races, in small or big scale, to bless themselves or to curse themselves. Regardless of the ups and downs of the worldly

drama of global events, the best contribution any individual
can make to assist the world is to work on his self-development and spiritual balance. This is as much as I know.

*Q: How does heaven, which is your term for the source of all
spirits, influence human nature with regard to destiny?*

Master Ni: Are you talking about individual destiny, or the
destiny of human life in totality?

Q: Well, they are tied together; that is my understanding.

Master Ni: You are answering greatly. However, at some level
they are tied together sometimes. You see, we have now
become two legged creatures with a brain and two skillful
arms and hands, different from all other animals. This is a
continuous evolution. Life itself, in a big sense, is not
individual. We are participating, we are joining, we are small
entities of the big universal life. The universe itself is gov-
erned by the subtle law. We do not need to worry about the
operation of the subtle law. A relevant question out of the
reflection of a spiritually aware person would be, "Did I do
anything foolishly against the subtle law," or "Did my small
group of friends or the majority of society do something
foolishly against the subtle law?" Without knowledge of the
subtle law, a person or group will do anything they wish, and
that brings trouble.

About personal destiny, or the destiny of the human
world, it takes spiritual development to know the subtle law
and understand destiny. The subtle law cannot be changed
by any strong leader or any lawmaker. It is always there. If
you and I ask, "What is my destination or destiny?", perhaps
the answer would be more specific about a small section of
your life, your healthy being, financial being or social being.
You do not need to ask other people about such things.

We would like to continue our endless evolution to
become better and better all the time. We are not going to
suffer all the time. No one enjoys suffering or making
mistakes again and again. People can think of making
personal progress for a better world. They dream of it, but in

reality they cannot achieve it, because they are using the tool wrongly or they are using the wrong tool. The foundation that they use to bring about their improvement is wrong too.

One mistake in their foundation is trying to make the external establishment satisfy their beliefs. In Chinese villages, children sometimes disobey their mother. Then when a storm comes and there is thunder and lightening, the mothers says, "God is angry because you disobeyed your parents." Or some parents say, "The boogeyman will get you." If a person relies on those things to teach their children, the children will never grow well.

When their baby cries, some foolish mothers do not stop him from crying by diverting his attention to something else of a positive nature. Instead, they tell their kids that the policeman will come to take them if they do not stop crying. The kids stop crying, but when they grow up, they start to shake when they see a policeman, even though they are not criminals. All of us are programmed in some way by our mother and father. Our parents also suffer from the programming of their parents. So we need to forgive them with love, and put our attention on changing our own destiny. Otherwise we will suffer the same things our parents did. Telling children that policemen will attack them if they misbehave only creates a psychological state of readiness for being controlled by a strong government or religion when the children grow into adults.

Becoming Tao is becoming nature. You need to deprogram all things and guard yourself from more contamination. With a natural being, you do not need to keep the artificial. When the healthy being of mind is restored, the rest of the aspects of one's life will be improved too.

Heaven, as I frequently use it, describes a good person, good people, a good place or the meeting of good people. It can be the second or the fifth line in a hexagram. It means a balance point. It can be a point where the public spirit and the individual interest meet together. It can be a point where the external and the internal one dissolve at the same time and place. Thus, heaven can be anywhere, any time and any people. To people of an undeveloped stage, heaven is their spiritual ambition. To people of spiritual development,

Heaven is a realization. My work is to invite all of you to join me to realize it. I choose this as my destiny. I also recommend this to be your destiny and that each person kick away the transient personal concerns of our daily life.

Q: My question is about members in the family and the traditional relationships of husband and wife, father and mother, sons and daughters, sisters and brothers. Do you see these relationships changing in modern times?

Master Ni: They are changing a lot. People have changed to become more selfish and more self protective from the difficulty of general worldly life. If people improve their practical lives and attain their spiritual growth, no one needs to go live in caves or nest in trees. I think our relationships still can be made. We need to find a particular solution for each situation. Perhaps you are going to find one!

Q: Will the problem of drug use and abuse in the world get better or worse?

Master Ni: We must not overlook the problem of drugs. Using drugs is similar to the use of alcohol or religion to support an emotion. Using drugs is a different faith, a different support for people disappointed in their life condition. They use drugs or religion because they believe that they need that support in their lives. Otherwise no one would pay the high price of drugs or donate so much to churches. I do not think it is totally reliable to expect a change by passing laws to stop drug use. More importantly than making laws, we need, individually and as a whole society, to attain spiritual growth so that the problem can be solved.

You ask me if the problem will become better or worse. That depends. If people attempt to solve it only through general education about health, I do not think that it can be greatly reduced. Maybe politically something will be better with the superficial world peace, but internally, what help have they provided to most people? What is the real faith or belief of these people in life? They do not have any faith; they are only looking to drugs or to alcohol to numb their minds.

The difference between learning Tao and general religion is that in learning Tao, you need to attain spiritual soberness. In contrast, the general or religious promotion is spiritual drunkenness. It is not much different than using drugs.

So now, maybe you have a deeper reaction to what I am saying, like, "Master Ni, spiritual soberness is not enjoyable. When I am more awake, I feel more pain." If you feel pain, it is because you did not clean up the emotional clouds in your head and chest. Thus, you do not see the clear direction of your life. But at the time that you attain the learning of Tao, you cannot say, "I am awake; let the whole world be drunk." No, a person is not happy if he lets the whole market use the false money and he alone uses the true gold. That cannot solve the problem.

To learn Tao you need to associate with good people; you need supportive and trustworthy friends. At least you will have a small scope of friends who are achieved and with whom you feel relaxed. Naturally you will come to trust each other's virtue in joining together to learn and develop our spiritual good flowers and fruit. Your spiritual group, at least, can help provide some support. You will not hurt them and they will not hurt you. But you need your alertness when you are in other environments to keep your balance.

By ourselves, we need to learn more and achieve more in our internal sufficiency and spiritual full development so that we do not rely on any cultural religious drugs, real alcohol or real drugs.

Q: In the process of self-cultivation, I often come across the problem of discerning what is the true mind. I always hear different voices, different things.

Master Ni: This is the first thing: you do not need to worry about it. You hear many voices because you have not had enough spiritual purification. This happens because of the invasion of the commercial culture and the murky social environment everyone lives in and grew up in. In such a setting, everyone must have experienced many voices. It is important to distinguish the voice to know which one it is; it is important to ignore all the mixed and confusing voices.

In the moment when you do not hear any voice, you are centered. By not fighting the external voice or any disturbance, you slowly center yourself and gather the best energy that is produced. But do not follow any voice. Any voice would be a trap. Thank you for your good question.

Q: The more that people reproduce, the worse the planet gets. Are there too many people?

Master Ni: We feel the pressure of more and more people everywhere. When people live too close, more friction is brought about, then people hate each other. Their tension is built up by the pressure of the closeness. People then become like porcupines. Once a wise person said, "Human nature is like this: if people live too far away, they feel cold. If they live too close together, then like porcupines, they sting each other." And definitely, because the world is overpopulated, this situation will degrade the quality of human people.

In our tradition, we say that there are usually two reasons that many people have lots of children. One is that they do not know how to manage themselves. Another is they do not understand that having a child is a high responsibility. Life is not just following the impulse of lovemaking for personal enjoyment by people who do not care about the quality of the people they are bringing into the world. That is not being responsible.

Also, let us talk about spiritual cultivation. If a person is looking for spiritual fitness or survival after death, his life will take a different direction than the person looking for general worldly accomplishment. The general good direction is people using their reproductive force to bring about the well being of their descendants in the world; it is not the ambition to give birth to so many children. A good descendent is reason for celebration. If it is a bad descendant, you suffer for your own impulsive creation.

Do you know the secret of our life? This may be a little deeper than you want to hear, but I will venture it. The family ghosts or spirits, which are usually the tiny spiritual energies of your relatives such as grandfather or grandmother, will live in the back part of your head. They cannot strongly affect your mind, but their influence is a part of your destiny. Sometimes when you feel sad or feel like crying, maybe it is not from your emotions, but from your spiritual source. There is no communication from them to you in the way of speech. They cannot pass their experience to you. They cannot teach you the wisdom that they have attained from the lessons of their lives.

It is not important how many children you bring into the world; what is important is self-achievement. Some people can be happily married; some people cannot. You need to live according to your own personal, individual differences. Some people can bring happy children into the world and some cannot. Even in those relationships which are good and happy, each person still needs to look separately for spiritual responsibility and the true benefit of having children.

All of you in this country know about some famous families that have lots of money. When the children are born, they are born with spoons made of silver and inlaid with diamonds in their mouths. But you can see that they suffer. The level of spiritual success is not a matter of how rich a person is and how many children one brings into the world; it is a spiritual practice to bring good children into the world.

Also, if by your personal destiny you are not happy being paired, then do not try. All your attempts will bring only failure and cause more trouble. It is not necessary to be paired in life. If you are not happy being paired and you are wise enough, you look for a different path in your life to work on yourself spiritually. In this lifetime, you can strengthen your soul. In case you reincarnate again; you can do it better. There are other higher spiritual choices too.

What is important for us to see is that now we are alive in the world. We must use the opportunity of our external life condition to improve our internal, spiritual condition in the body house. We need to protect that house. The whole world is a house too. And when you look things over again, you see that the whole world is a life too. The achieved Taoists say that human life is still in the stage of a child. Even though human life has passed through several billion years of evolution, it has not grown too much. All people have a group of spirits within them; some special people's inner spirits have attained their growth. Some never attain growth. Thus, they cannot expect to do right or say right all the time. It is the same thing in the big society: no one can expect all individuals or the majority to grow to the same height and wisdom. What is the difference among people? The big difference among people is the degree to which they have developed spiritually.

To learn Tao is to achieve ourselves integrally, not partially. It is not excusable for a Taoist student to become irresponsible with his life being. Our responsibility is to attain our full spiritual growth and help those people we can reach. Some people, even if they live in the same house, cannot accept such communication. If you experience that, do not be troubled. Recognize it and accept it and work only to improve yourself. Teaching by example is louder and more convincing than words.

Q: What does it mean to purify your energy, and how do we know what thoughts and behavior we need to purify?

Master Ni: Most people are a mixture of energy. Spiritually, each person does not like some things. It is not you who creates some of the life experiences which you do not like to have; the external world forces you to experience them. Maybe you drive your car well and watch carefully on the way, but somebody else might hit you because of his drinking, drugs or irresponsible way of driving. Then you are troubled, and you react. Your emotional reaction of anger or resentment is combined with the rough or unpleasant external experience. Both the experience and the emotion punish you. Let us say that you have been working on your development and have grown some. Then you might think, "How can this have happened to me? I am spiritual. I am a good person." However, a good person is not necessarily always fortunate. Accidents happen unintentionally; one should not make a mental burden out of them. Purity is something different than what happens externally in your life. Purity is subjective effort in attaining soul protection.

On the general level, there are more good people than bad people. Emotionally, some people react strongly, weakly, not at all or they greatly overreact. Your emotions, mental reactions and thoughts are all gathered from external experience and become you. For example, if you have grown up in a rough neighborhood, your experiences may have led you to become cruel or insensitive in your actions. Once your self knowledge grows, you will know what areas you need to improve. However, in our life, whether it be the deep sphere or shallow sphere, the mind always needs to know clearly whether we behave correctly and react well enough to each situation.

Here is an illustration of incorrect or unclear behavior. Let us say that you are a married person and in a situation in which you become angry over something that your wife has done. Perhaps you cannot express your anger directly because your wife is too strong or communication between you is not so good. So you express it to your kids. Or, in another example, sometimes a person's boss says something unkind and the person gets upset. Then he goes home and treats his wife unkindly. It happens. People transfer their anger or resentment, not remembering who was the object of the anger to begin with. Some people are confused all the time. They have not clearly understood with their minds.

So purification is important. It is a daily process. What is purification? Any time someone comes to you, whether their influence is good, bad or neutral, immediately, once you are alone or at the right occasion or right time, you purify yourself without letting the people or the experience poison or influence you. You free yourself of the result of that interaction. This is at the shallower level.

In the deeper level, the book called *The Heavenly Way*, which is reprinted as *The Key to Good Fortune: Refining Your Spirit*, can help you. My books might serve as an example. The attainment of the knowledge of oneself and applying spiritual purification to yourself will be beneficial to you.

Q: Could you discuss the influence of Taoism in China.

Master Ni: That is a good question. Taoism has already come back in China, but under a different name. Forty years ago, the Chinese Communist leaders were young. They imported the formula of Communism and the immature thought of materialism from other parts of the world. They believed that formula could save China and make people live better, so they destroyed all the good things and the achievement of the ancient people.

Now they have become old. They are already disillusioned by their discovery that Communism cannot save China, but only cause more trouble. The reality is that they were not mature enough when they imported Communism into China. They have organized things so that everybody can say, "We are treated equally; you are paid the same amount of money and I am also paid the same amount of money." But what is not publicized is, "I am a member of the party and I have extra treats secretly that people do not know about." Most of the people have suffered, but the few people who work in the party enjoy special privilege. Even their special enjoyment, however, is less than that of the ordinary worker who lives in a free and developed society. Even if he owns a poor car, it can still be repaired; he has fewer work hours and can go anywhere. The people in China cannot enjoy that much.

The main point is not to talk about Communism. They were too young to know the value of the ancient achieved ones. Now, after forty years, they have become old, and what is left for them? They are asking, "Can I live healthily? Can I live enjoyably? Can I live fully, with the love of other people?" Especially, they are asking, "Can I live longer?" Okay, let us say that they have those desires. Communism cannot fulfill those desires for them. So now they are looking for the traditional treasure: the learning of Tao. The secrets are coming back under the title of "Chi Kung" (Chi Gong). Chi Kung is Taoism. T'ai Chi Movement is Taoism. It is not a Communist creation. The majority of people are coming back to it.

More interesting is that the intellectuals doubted the historical record about the many immortals and their magic powers. Now they trust it. Why? Because they see many children and adults who have no association with the old culture yet who have a natural gift of all kinds of special powers. It is marvelous. For example, many children can read by ear. Some of them read by moving their fingers on the flat surface of paper. Many children can hear another person's mind. That type of thing started to appear again more than ten years ago, after the cultural revolution was over. Now the government leaders come back to see that many people have different powers. Now the government is conducting many important tests. Once a group of doctors and the important figures of the government sat around a table. On the table there was a glass bottle containing a few red pills; the bottle was sealed. One person in another room then used his mind to take the pills out of the bottle. The government has trusted the so-called materialism; if they were to be more objective and go deeper into study, they would need to revise their theories of how things work.

Those power demonstrations are still shallow performances. There is also a marvelous healing power that makes many things happen which modern medicine cannot explain.

The subtle law states that when a person comes to the extreme bad side, he has to change or otherwise, he will totally destroy himself. There is no argument; it is a fact of life. Let us rephrase that in Taoist terms of philosophy: when yang comes to the extreme, it turns into yin. When yin comes to the extreme, it comes to be yang. They always play seesaw. The human world moves like that. Only the ones who attain spiritual awakening keep their focus on staying centered and moving in a healthy direction. But the blind world vigorously shifts from one side to the other. On one side, they feel dangerous and they go back to the other side. Then when the other side is too much and feels dangerous, they move back to the first side. They are never really balanced. This is why in my teaching, I will ask all of you to pay attention to what you are going to achieve. Be centered. There is a certain safe scope in which one can move along, but never go over the margins into danger.

Q: In the Taoist tradition, is there an initiation procedure, and if so, how does that help the individual in his spiritual cultivation and to help others spiritually?

Master Ni: It depends on the individual. If the individual is ready, the teaching really works. It can save the person tens of years of cultivation, maybe several lifetimes of cultivation. If the student is not ready, at least it makes the connection. I will authorize Maoshing to help you open your spiritual channels as a spiritual service. But it is not a negative commandment: "You must be a student of the tradition of Tao." We give this service so you can enjoy. Becoming a Taoist is not a committed obligation to anyone but yourself.

If you do not have any more questions, I would now like Maoshing to do the spiritual initiation; to initiate you to do your own pursuit of spiritual cultivation and development. I have provided all the books; I hope my books and teachings provide the explanation and the description to assist in your achievement and attainment.

Anyone who wishes to be initiated and to have their channels opened, please come forward. Your hands should be held this way, higher and central. The lower abdomen is the sexual center; you might already have enough energy there so move your hands up and put them over your heart.

Beloved friends, a short talk hardly gives a complete message of my teaching. Asking and answering questions cannot concentrate on what all of us wish to reach. However, an individual human life contains the truth of the entire universe. The spiritual growth of an individual includes the complete history of all religions. You are welcome to be my friends. Let us work together and share our growth with each other in order to attain the total growth of people and the entire society of mankind.

An individual human life contains the truth of the entire universe. The spiritual growth of an individual includes the complete history of all religions. Thank you.

Chinese New Year Observance In Atlanta,
at the Center for Taoist Arts
February 12, 1989

Chapter 3

Who is Able to Play Such a Big Game?

Q: Master Ni, please tell us of the high achievements. Is it a different kind of achievement when the soul exuviates and the body remains seated in a meditative position? Or when the soul returns to the body after several days? Or when some small pearl-like stones are left behind? Perhaps those types of exuviation are made by less achieved souls but are still of greater achievement than the general public.

Master Ni: The technique whereby an achieved soul perfectly withdraws from its body is called exuviation. The higher achievement is to dissolve its body and become vaporized during the time of physically leaving the world. In the many instances of this type of exuviation, there might be only some hair and fingernails left. The soul flies away with the refined new life and is seen as a shooting rainbow. An even higher way than that is to ascend with the physical body; it rises to the sky, flying on its way towards its destiny. By the change of environment, it quits its physical shape, bit by bit, until it is pure spirit. I mean, it dissolves its physical shape little by little until it is pure spirit. This is called wholly ascending. This achievement was mentioned less frequently in the Taoist historical records - the Taoists were not an organized institution - and in the historical records of the lands where these events actually happened.

Whatever the way of ascending, the world is no longer of interest to the soul. The soul has entered a new stage of life. There is no more work, but only pure being in a range which fits the achievement of the soul. The person's name may still be used in religious activities or in channeling or magic writing. However, rarely does the true spirit of the person reappear in the case of magic writing or channeling. Mostly these phenomena are a general spiritual reflection of the channel rather than a reappearance of the true soul or the original soul.

Q: Thank you for your answer. However, if I may, I would like to ask the question again.

Master Ni: Now I am talking about the game of death. Because we are talking about the game of death, we must also talk about the game of life. Let us discuss them.

I do not know how many people make a game of death. Death is something imposed on a person; nobody can refuse its coming. There is not much of a game to play or anything interesting about it for most people. But when I talk about the game of death in connection with the Taoists, there is lots of play. What I mean is, the Taoists make a game out of life and death. They do not take either subject, life or death, too seriously; they find much enjoyment in them. Let us now focus on the people with independent spirit called Taoists, who play life and death.

Let us talk about the game of life. I need to tell you a secret. I wonder if I should tell you or not. . . I had better tell you, otherwise you will ask too much. You know, in the world the most powerful thing is the childlike heart. I repeat: a child's heart is the most powerful thing. Whatever he wants in his mind, such as what he wants to be, what he wishes to own, whom he wants to marry and what kind of life he desires, are all planted like a seed within him. A child's heart plants the wish; in other words, the desire is planted in that pure heart. I tell you this: the world must give way to him. It is true. The life of many adults are the fulfillment or achievement of the desire from the child's heart.

When I was a child, I did not know that my heart was so powerful. If I had known that then, I could have better organized my heart to desire what to be, what to have, who to marry and so forth. A child's heart mostly expresses the natural inclination of the child. In the deep heart of a child, he does what he wants. So in the later part of his life, he goes to fulfill what he wished for. Perhaps you did not know that when you were a child, you wrote the play that you are now playing. You are now the adult. No matter what age you are, 20, 30, 40, or even older, 70 or 80, you are still playing. You are a player, an actor, acting out the drama written by yourself as a child. Most people never know that. So we are being played; we are being managed by the child's heart.

Here is another secret of life: there are two kinds of childlike heart. The first kind is a child who has a soul with a background. The soul may have something that was unfulfilled in its past lives, so it has returned to the world and taken a flesh body to accomplish that fulfillment. Ordinary people or general souls live that type of life. Just like the child who wrote the play for itself, this type of life is prewritten. It is already formed in advance.

Now I would like to talk about the second and more powerful kind of child's heart, which is the unformed child's heart. Generally speaking, all the children's hearts are formed. The unformed child's heart is rare and special.

Now I will take a deep breath for fresh air, then give you another secret: each individual has an internal form. I mean, when a person is a child, usually the internal shape is already decided. It is pre-decided if the person will be a banker, be the bandit who robs the bank, be in the government and so on. It is an internal shape. When a person appears before the eyes of an achieved Taoist, he can see the internal shape there. The shape is so small, it is a tiny little bit of thing in the center of the mind of the person. But that grows to take over the whole life.

Let me come back to talk about the unformed child's heart. The unformed childlike heart is most powerful; it is close to Tao. You can directly call it Tao, the unformed power. Let me tell you this: most Taoists live with an unformed heart. What is it like to have an unformed childlike heart? Whatever happens, the Taoist enjoys. He is not choosy, he is not picky.

The formed child heart, on the other hand, rejects whatever he does not know or like. He may not even know why he does not like the thing, but he will refuse to approach whatever he does not want to approach. You see, most things were decided by people when they were children. It is as though the child draws a blueprint from which he never strays. It is already decided in the blueprint if he is going to love this thing and hate that thing. It makes him a puppet for the blueprint that was decided so long ago by a small child.

Most of the time, if something comes to his hand that is not what he expected or had previously accepted, he automatically dislikes it. He hates it, is bored with it, or is troubled by it, so he is unhappy. Some people's lives are 50% unhappy and 50% happy. Some are 70% unhappy and 30% happy. Some people are even more picky than that. On a Chinese feast table, for example, there are generally about 30 dishes. Some people may only like one dish or only a little bit of one dish, while others may like all of them. But there are those who are unhappy with maybe 29 dishes, or maybe even all of them: the dish they like has not been served yet!

However, to the person with an unformed Taoist childlike heart, all of the dishes, whatever they are, make him happy. He is simply happy. Each moment for a Taoist is like that: good is happy, bad is happy, to have a lot makes him happy, to have none also makes him happy. Gain is happy, loss is happy. There is no way to make him unhappy, although sometimes, it takes a few minutes for the Taoist to make a new adjustment. Whatever happens, he is happy. That is really a powerful, indestructible child heart. It is the most divine, most angelic and a most respectable way to live. That does not mean that he does not make choices. His pure and strong spirit makes the right choice directly, without intellectual interpretation. Also, he may not appear to show the happiness he feels inside all of the time. Happiness is a not really a feeling. Happiness is to be.

Twice I spent some time in summer on Orcas Island in Washington State. I lived among the evergreen trees in a comfortable house. One day while I was on a walk, I found some bones of a deer. I lived close to the deer, thus I knew something about the way deer live. Deer do not make a nest like birds or people. They just walk around until their physical body fails, then they just lay down to die there. Taoists, when they live, according to the ancient record, are just like deer: deer are happy here, happy there, jumping everywhere, so happy, so curious. They do not care what happens, they just fix it and go on with their lives. They are happy everywhere, because they are the natural life force. Surely there is no book written about a deer disappointed in love.

On that island, there are no big animals except humans. They are not allowed to kill deer. The description of the deer is the description of how a Taoist lives with the power of innocence. The power of innocence is what Taoists pursue. I have used deer as an example to illustrate the free spirit of all natural life. Just like a deer, the Taoist walks everywhere; he does not say here is better or there is better in a judgmental way. He goes wherever he likes to go. I do not know if a deer knows when it is going to die. When its death comes, it does not know it is death. It does not even know it is a deer. A deer cannot help its own life to be different. Deer do not have philosophical development. Deer accept whatever is happening in their lives.

Similarly, a human life cannot assist destiny. But humans lie about death and thus create religions. People think they are smarter than deer. Deer accept the reality of nature as deer. However, it is doubtful that humans are wiser than deer, because so many humans cannot even accept the reality of their own lives. Nor do they live naturally like the deer. Truthfully, people cannot do anything to alter their destiny with the advantages and shortcomings of their innate nature. Even their complicated emotions are used to create false cultures of religion, which lie to their psychology.

In giving you the example of the life of a deer, I am not teaching you in any way to live exactly like a deer. People cannot do that. People have lost their opportunity to be happy deer, to live on a vast, natural and safe range. My message to you is not to be happy deer, it is to be happy humans. Although the pattern has become set so that each one of us needs to win the battle of life, that is not nature's intent. It has been intensified by our own creation. That is not what I am talking about. I am saying that the most powerful thing in each human life is the power of natural life. Unfortunately, that delightful natural light has been designated as a secondary culture, religion or politics by those who do not understand it.

As humans, we are now all culturally programmed. We are taught to like only one word: life. We are taught to greatly dislike another word: death. But whether we like the word "death" or not, that dish is also served.

To return to our other topic, those Taoists who live with an unformed child heart do not have a predetermined play or a written drama for them to act out. Therefore, they live with a vast range of things to enjoy. Their lives are not narrowed down like people who have a written drama that must be exactly acted out according to that plan. They live a different kind of life. Because he is not trying to conform himself to a certain fixed idea, the life spirit of the Taoist is not damaged.

I would like to give you an illustration of how a person's life spirit comes to be damaged. Let us make a metaphor. A beautiful, sharp sword that is used to cut all kinds of things, even stones and metal, will end up having notches and dents all over the blade. The blade becomes dull and damaged. An ordinary human life does not know where to go to use its resources or abilities effectively; it hits or cuts everywhere trying to find its way. When people are born and when they are youngsters, their life is as sharp as a freshly ground sword, but by using it emotionally or blindly instead of wisely, they cut in unsuitable places. In the end, they cause the beautiful sword to become notched. So many people damage themselves by applying their ambitions, desires, wants or loves too intensely, which results in disappointment, emotional pain or injuries: all are notches on their sword. At times there are other, external reasons why they become notched. Some people are notched deeply, while others are not so deeply notched. Sometimes the spirit has wounds everywhere, from top to bottom. If the spirit is an old wolf, he sits there, licking all the wounds he received from his big fights with all the other wolves. Maybe he even fought with bears.

But the one who is not pre-programmed cuts nothing, and therefore hurts nothing, keeps his soul complete and maintains the freshness of life. When he dies, he is not worn out. His spirit is still strong, so the exuviation that happens to this person is different. Thus, when he comes here he is complete, and when he goes away he is complete. He has correctly used his life (his sword); he is complete. His spirit is not like the sword that was used too much or used wrongly and is damaged at the end.

Most people die feeling worn out at the end of their life. The souls of untroubled children and young people are usually stronger than worn out adult souls. Having a worn out soul is not a good example of how to live. These people like to live like a hero, fight like a hero, win or be defeated like a hero and die hard like a hero. In their lifetime, they have not learned to nurture their spirit at all. Typically, at the end of their life, because they are so worn down, they want out. They want to die. We do not like to talk about that too much, however, because that is not what we would like for people. I wish that everybody would live happily and be over a hundred years old. So let us talk about living to be over a couple of hundred years old.

We must speak of the quality as well as the quantity of life. We need to enjoy each minute. Then, if a person lives to be over 100 years old, being here for so long is a great blessing. However, if a person does not enjoy each minute, and he lives to be over 100 years old, then I would say that each minute is a punishment. You can see that life is quantity and quality together.

Taoists pursue immortality. Some Taoists who did not study enough on their own may not even know the word immortality; they just know that their life has the happy quality to it that we described before.

Taoists basically do not damage themselves. Cultivation with the purpose of nurturing their spiritual energy is one word that can describe their activity, but, they do not damage their spirit by internal or external fighting all the time. You see, in a fight, if a person is defeated, his soul will have an invisible scar. He suffers from being cut by people. But also on the other hand, if he is the winner, he may gather lots of hatred, so winning is bad for your soul also. Either way, a person damages himself. Competition is not spiritual culture.

Now we return to talk about the Taoist who plays death. How does he play death? Many times it was written in the records that when a Taoist died, people would bury him in a coffin. Sometime later, then, he would appear elsewhere or in several different places. The people who buried him would begin to doubt that he was dead, and when they would go to check it out, they would discover an empty coffin. Taoists often do this.

Oh yes, one more thing. People who are notched and wounded, if they have not damaged themselves too much, can heal their own spiritual wounds just as the physical body heals its own cuts and scratches. I have written about other lifestyles and practices in my other books.

Now you may ask your question.

Q: Does the type of exuviation depend on how a person achieves himself spiritually? You mentioned some high ones and I would like you to talk about the different types.

Master Ni: After religions began to promote it, people began to think that sitting meditation was holy. People think that meditation must be done correctly and effectively during one's life to cultivate the soul, and continued during death as the way to go. Some Taoists accept that, but others do not. In the later generations after the religious conception was established, because people came to think that meditation was a generally acceptable form of spiritual cultivation, when a person died in sitting meditation, they believed he ascended. That is not necessarily true.

Human life activity can usually be divided into several categories. One type is being wholly awake. A second type is being wholly asleep. A third way is not being awake or asleep, but dreaming. A fourth is being in a kind of light consciousness; it is not sleep or dreaming, nor is it being awake either. It is not wholly concentrating on doing work or doing anything. In this range of consciousness, there are different practices that can be done. Some unachieved meditators meditate in a way that is stiff, with no thinking or dreaming. The Taoist way is different; we can called it tipsiness, or brewing the sweet, clear and light energy so that it rises to one's head. Thus, the Taoist cultivates a peaceful joy which is indescribable. It is not being asleep, awake, drunk or dreaming, nor is it a stiffening religious meditation of holding oneself in a tight, non-thinking mood. It is being spiritually tipsy. It is a kind of bliss he experiences all the time. While he is walking, he can be tipsy. He can do things with tipsy, eat with tipsy, sleep with tipsy, talk with tipsy; it is not only in meditation that he nurtures that kind of life energy. It is brewed by all the things that he does like Chi Kung (Chi Gong), T'ai Chi Movement, walking, breathing practice, and even in everyday life. So it cannot necessarily be said that only when a person is seated in meditation that he is holy, cultivating himself, or spiritual.

Q: But the gentleman you once told us about did die sitting up in a meditation posture.

Master Ni: I believe you refer to Mr. Koo. He is different. That is why we cannot totally deny it. But meditation is not the only way to reach for achievement. There are different things that a person can do. Meditation is one important aspect or thing that can help a person gather himself to become one piece, when a person practices it correctly.

Our friend had his practice, and he needed to teach his sons by example. His sons are somewhat worldly people. At least because of their father's achievement, they must think, "My father spent his whole lifetime studying Tao. We must look at the result." I think that gentleman did splendidly.

It is true as people believe that some achieved souls leave behind some crystallized stones when the body is burned at death.

Q: Or pearls, like Buddhists have?

Master Ni: Yes, those too. But I think it is not necessary to make that proof of one's spiritual achievement. I think that Chinese Buddhism, especially Zahn (Zen) Buddhism, is a transformed Taoist tradition which adopted a different outer garment but does not necessarily agree that is correct practice. Any spiritually achieved person, Zahn Buddhist, Taoist or other, whose life is not such a serious matter as it is for most people, knows that it is not necessary for him to leave some crystal stones behind when he dies to prove his achievement to people. To him, that is a silly thing, which would bring laughter. It is more a way for the regular religious leaders or promoters to encourage or attract people to follow them.

Q: So they tell them those things or do those things so that people will begin to think differently about their lives, right?

Master Ni: Yes, but if people keep looking for proof of achievement, this is spiritual unachievement, undevelopment or ungrowth. In Zahn Buddhism, when the masters go through their exuviation, some sit and others stand. Some even stand on their head or on one foot or in any funny way! To them, life is a play. They do such outrageous things because their whole life is quiet, and they know that the alive people want to see some fun. So they do it for show. Surely there are lots of Taoist who live quietly and who also pass from their bodies quietly, not trying to make people curious at anything.

Q: So they die in a way that is completely ordinary, right? And nobody knows at all that they were highly achieved.

Master Ni: They die just the same way that they lived, making no special show. So you see, all the display is unnecessary. But I tell you, as students, as modern people, that as we live in the world, either we are fulfilling the written drama of the developed child heart, or we are living with an unformed child heart.

In my case, I think I have a purpose in coming to the world; I accepted the challenge of the epoch changing from the old to the new development. I believe that other highly achieved ones are not challenged by the world at all; they know the world must learn through its own growth, through its own problems. They think, "It is not my problem; why should I come back to the world to suffer for that?"

However, it is important to know to appreciate the unformed heart, and also to know that each individual has an internal form or shape. If a person wishes to shape himself, he can reform or dissolve his internal shape. Once he dissolves the internal form or shape, he is free. We suffer from bondage, but not necessarily external bondage; most bondage is internal bondage. The bondage comes from the pre-Heaven stage; a person brings whatever spiritual defect he has with him into the world when he is born. Spiritual cultivation does away with or abolishes the spiritual defect. We work hard spiritually to dissolve the shape or form of whatever is inside of us. Then we can regain the freedom that we once knew.

Cultivation also means not building any more bondage for our soul. Each day in the world, we learn more in a practical way of the world's knowledge. In doing so, however, we usually bring more bondage to ourselves. The healthy spiritual model of the ancient achieved ones was this: they had an unformed child heart and so were happy each minute. They were happy, not crazy; they accommodated the world situation without creating or programming bondage for themselves. Even external bondage did not hurt them at all; they still enjoyed whatever form the world could present. Even in a situation of living under Communism, some people still do better, while other people suffer more. The Communist leaders especially suffer; they follow external formality to establish the argument and then they enter combat, not only mentally but also physically. Then finally, they ruin each other. Nobody is the winner. They are still following the law of the jungle, the animalistic level of life.

From this discussion, we can understand something of life itself. If a person calls this moment life, then, they are calling the last moment death. A person cannot truthfully say, "In the future, I am going to die," because each person, at each moment, is in the process of both living and dying. Each moment is to die and to live. Most undeveloped people think life and death are separated things. They do not know they are in the process of doing both in each moment. They do not realize that each moment they are given a great opportunity for a better life, because they are not awake enough to see it and take advantage of it. They only look for change when they die. They expect a better life next time, as religions commonly promote. General religions say that people will be judged, rewarded or punished, and that it will occur some time later. Taoists say, in each moment you are given the opportunity to live a better life, if you decide to.

So, as the beloved friends of my teaching, do you decide to take advantage of that opportunity or do you keep worrying about when you are going to die? Let me tell you this: you are not going to die, you are going to move. You are going to transform spiritually from one stage to a higher stage. That is what death is all about. Before you came to the world, you lived without a flesh form. Now that you have come to the world, you live with a flesh form. The experiences from the new life teach you. You take essence from the learning of the new life and in that way you evolve. Your new spirit is not the original one. It is new life. Through transformation, exuviation or ascending, you grow to a new stage.

Once you view life differently, you also view death differently. Most people view life as eating, sexing, enjoying money, having power, and they think they are only living when they do or have those things. A spiritual student, on the other hand, knows that the value of each minute is not measured by those things; it is measured by the amount of spiritual freedom he has. He constantly asks himself, "Do I create bondage for myself by what I do, say, promise or by how I work?" An ordinary person without spiritual education continues to create more bondage for himself. His life is like a flying dragon that gets caught in the network of a spider's web. The more it struggles, the stronger the bondage becomes.

In the spiritual world, there are no spider webs, and there is no flying dragon. There is only you, the child who has written everything for itself. When you learn that it is you who creates the drama of your life by what you think, say and do, then you wish to learn how to manage yourself better and so begin to change. Everything a person writes is for himself.

Because the majority of people who are interested in religion are concerned mostly about the topic of death, I think I like to offer some other information about that from my knowledge.

There are lots of Taoists who escape from their coffins after people put them in there following their death. That is no strange thing. They play that for certain, but I do not know for what crazy reason they do it. Most of them do it to stop people from admiring them and loving them, because they have stayed in one place too long and earned too much love and appreciation from people. Most people love to be treated with warmth, sweetness and love. A Taoist thinks that to rely on that good treatment would be poison to his righteous characteristics. Thus, to play death is a way of getting rid of the spider's web. However, the behavior of a Taoist cannot be predicted. One master called Wang Tzung Yen, who started the northern sect of religious Taoism, I believe was an achieved person. He did not die old; he was around the age of 59. He enjoyed high respect and had many followers. Thus, as I see, he decided to not to stay around too long to deal with that, so he died. After he died, he was going to be buried in a different county. Many students were needed to carry the coffin to the new burial place. Do you know what trick this Taoist played? There were a great many admirers on each stop along the funeral route who offered sacrifice and showed their respects. Those people, and the students who had a true heart to cultivate themselves, smelled the sweet fragrance of the most expensive incense. The other ones, who mingled in the group, and those who were not true nor good students, experienced an odor like dead fish. It was the same smell, but for different people, there was a different enjoyment.

Q: Do you mean that the smell came from the coffin?

Master Ni: Yes, from the coffin, the whole way while they transported it. It was not only the students who experienced it, but it also affected some of the people on the roadside. The good people all smelled a sweet fragrance, but others did not. Many people came along to watch the big parade and smelled that. I think this is a typical game of death he played that is worthy of mention here.

Q: Does a person have to be highly achieved in an earthly sense to be a highly achieved Taoist? In other words, usually the people that you hear about that are highly achieved people are born into special families, have long illustrious careers as healers and are great and famous spiritual leaders. I think it is wondrous. But does a person have to be highly achieved like that to be highly achieved as a Taoist?

Master Ni: No, what you are talking about is destiny. You are talking about an external thing, not about spiritual achievement at all. Spiritual achievement has no connection with destiny or external happenings at all. Spiritual virtue can accumulate a good foundation of life and freedom, but freedom cannot be contained in any form. All the forms are too small to confine or contain that freedom.

Now I need to change the subject a little bit. How do the Taoists achieve high immortality and ascension? Do you want to know about that?

Q: Yes.

Master Ni: I do not hesitate to talk about it. It is totally unlike what the regular religions promote. Mostly Taoists play energy, not immature psychology. There have been three ways of spiritual achievement in attaining immortality.

The first way, was the way of a king or a queen; this type of achievement mostly occurred before the world became totally populated and civilized like today. Life was still natural and uncomplicated in that time. The king or queen, or other capable men or women, used sexual encounters with a great number of the opposite sex, and were perhaps benefitted by those opportunities. They achieved longevity and immortality. The knowledge of this heritage still exists. However, I do not think that the new world has the proper conditions for that type of practice or for attaining spiritual achievement in that way.

The second way was developed much later, more than two thousand years ago. Society shifted from its natural way to a strong, authoritative government by monarchies. Because of the restrictive and dangerous nature of the new governmental controls, people of spiritual interest withdrew from society to live in mountains, forests and rural places to do their spiritual cultivation. These people mostly achieved by themselves without external support or sexual benefit. This is the hard way. However, the principle is the same, so people can also achieve themselves by self-spiritual integration.

The third way is the way that I continue in my tradition: to live in the world and cultivate oneself at the same time. We are not kings or queens who have all kinds of special opportunities. Nor do we totally become hermits in the mountains; we live a life close enough to the world to obtain some of its benefits and disadvantages as well, not far enough away to be separated from its customs and restrictions. However, we live with spiritual independence. We live among people. We serve people as well as allow people to serve us. We grow with people. Yet we do not choose the same growth as the worldly people. We particularly choose to grow correctly and to be as good as we can. If we can share our growth and understanding with people, we do so.

There are secrets in Taoist practice, like the reintegration of the life energy, directly by an individual himself or by someone involved with the opposite gender, but this is not the sole practice. Because there is a lot of information taught about sexual techniques which some people call Tao, people mistakenly think that engaging in sexual activity as much as they can will make them immortal. However, these sexual techniques are not on the level of higher goals like immortality; they are nothing more than a different way to sexual satisfaction. These practices do not create anything real or lasting.

Truthful spiritual self-integration is considered by some to be a difficult road. It is not a path of fantasy or glamour. There are some practices involving sexual harmonization, but these require special knowledge and certain circumstances. Most of these practices are done within the context of a healthy, ongoing relationship between a man and woman, and are not even sexually oriented; they are spiritual in nature. Most practices involving sexual exchange are not as easy as individual self-integration, which is the integration of the natural energy within one individual. This is why I do not recommend them; why take the hard road when it is simpler to take the easy road?

However, it is written in many books that it is the integration of male and female energies that brings about Taoist immortality. It is true that the two energies of different genders are involved, but there is a beneficial guideline that can be used to fit all people. These guidelines are illustrated in my work, *The Story of Two Kingdoms.*

Q: So then a person does not have to become a famous healer or a famous teacher to become achieved?

Master Ni: No, a famous character may be a fake.

Q: But I am talking about the real ones.

Master Ni: No, to be achieved, a person does not have to be a real one either. An achieved one can be anybody.

Q: So anybody can do it?

Master Ni: In ancient times, sometimes they would discover the achieved ones among the loafers. Some of them did not have any stable job. So it is true that sometimes, but not always, the spiritually achieved ones or shiens, were what you might call a loafer. They did not necessarily have any fixed job or name; they did not have any fixed anything, like a relationship, for example. They could not be defined; so it was out of their wisdom, not out of inability, that they chose that type of lifestyle. In certain circumstances, they performed their powers to help people; but they immediately denied the gratitude by going away because they did not even wish to establish earning any respect. Respect was still another kind of bondage to them.

True achievement is different from the world's conception about achievement. Most people in the world consider themselves achieved when they have made a name for themselves, have a good position in society or have become a respectable person. An achieved shien, however, is different: his achievement is not related to how other people see him or what somebody gives him such as a position or respect. He actually does not want to be in a position for other people to give him anything. He just does whatever he likes to do; it is absolute freedom. A person's growth determines whether that is a suitable way of life or not.

Ordinary people, however, need something ready like a product on the market to make use of; this is why religious teaching is so powerful and influential for many people. To the truly spiritual students, religion is not the kind of thing they are looking for. They are looking for true spiritual achievement. There is nothing higher than one's own spiritual nature. Thus, truthful spiritual people do not put themselves in any kind of place or rank, where any judgement or competition would start about who is higher and who is lower. Not that.

Q: Then as I have understood from the teachings in all of your books, a Taoist can really be a person with any kind or degree of world achievement. Lao Tzu, if I understand correctly, worked in the governmental library or archives until he retired his position there. I suppose the worldly challenge had disturbed the peace of his life.

So then, true achievement is not based on material possessions, race, gender or social status at all. Religious rituals do not approach it, although for some people, religions begin to point them in the right direction. It also does not require a monastic lifestyle, totally restricted diet or years of perfected exercise like yoga, although those things can be helpful to one's healthy life and can serve as a foundation for achievement. Nor does true achievement have to do with sexual ecstacy, healing others, reading books and acquiring knowledge, being a saint, practicing shamanism, or the magic performance of energy play. I suppose, however, that many people's path of understanding is to learn how to handle and use those things so that they know the limitation of those things. All of those things are temporal or changing.

However, I seem to be a slow student. I have not yet been able to figure out what is unchanging. I am not sure I want you to tell me. I think I have to figure it out myself. It is true, though, you do save us a lot of time by telling us things. Otherwise we would waste lots of time and energy looking in the wrong direction.

Maybe a person's mind can never figure it out; it is just something you have to do and be.

Master Ni: There are many things a wise teacher does not say. He would just let people grow tall enough to see whatever is on the other side of the boundary. As for myself, I say it. The reservation of the other wise teachers came from their own good reasons. People who do not grow enough need a certain form or attraction to make them become good and do good. In my case, I will ask my students to be good and do good without that kind of secondary attraction. I am not going to say, you drink the bitter, healing Chinese herb tea, and I will give you some candy afterwards. The benefit of doing good and being good is direct. Either a person will listen to it or not. This is why teaching attitudes, mine and those of the conventional teacher, are different. They have reservations. I do not; I do not think I should continue to reserve the truthful knowledge. If I reserve it, then the cunning-minded ones continue to play in their exploration to find out what I do not tell. That results in spiritual confusion; the untruthful teaching will continue to be taught by those who have not yet become achieved. Then the passing of truth only becomes an isolated island of one teacher to one student or of one teacher to a few students. If that continues, what is the help to the world?

In this discussion, if you are not ready for the deep exploration, you may be discouraged. If you are ready, you will stand stronger in your spiritual learning. This is why the wise ones before me were so careful about teaching the truth, because they did not want to say too much and to do too much for people who need to grow by themselves. I think the truth must be taught. Otherwise, when people grow, how will they be able to confirm what has been their true growth? They might not realize that it is true maturity that they have reached.

II

Q: Master Ni, after one's exuviation, if one does not vaporize one's body, what is spiritually correct to do with it? Somehow I feel that is important. In some places the custom is to bury it, in others to burn it. I suppose those different customs arose depending on the climatic environments, but spiritually, what is correct? Perhaps the spiritually correct thing to do is to follow the regional custom!

Master Ni: Some people do not accomplish the preparation of exuviation. Thus, there is a practice for the soul after physical failure. One can continue to do the spiritual integration in seven or forty-seven days. At most, the person's practice can extend to three years while the corpse lies in a coffin or underground. This practice is traditionally called "Forming oneself in the Yin sphere" (太陰煉形). This is ambiguous practice, it is the last chance. However, it is better to accomplish one's spiritual cultivation while one is alive, surely and methodically. Then, the hull, I mean the body, of the soul is safe to be burnt and the ash can be thrown into the ocean or a chosen place. The physical function, then, is totally accomplished.

Q: I am interested in the topic of death as well as the topic of life. The external way a person can die, such as sitting, standing, leaving pearl-like stones, ascending, walking out from the coffin, etc., are all interesting. However, more than that, I have strong interest in the spiritual knowledge about the transformation of physical life which is called death. Is there some spiritual knowledge that can be communicated by words that can guide a person through death, just as your words are helpful to guide us through life?

Master Ni: At that time, a good soul will find itself in a situation with sufficient protection to accomplish the practice called, "Tai Yin Lian Shing," which means "the refining spiritual formation in the stage of extreme yin." It is done by keeping the coffin in a dry, warm, fair southern place with exposure to the light of the sun, moon and stars. The coffin must be kept absolutely away from any disturbance. This is done after death.

There are four ranks of the fruit of spiritual cultivation in this matter.

The first correct fruit is the light and lightened flying soul.

The second correct fruit is the peaceful soul swimming in the light, nurtured as the future seeds of life.

The third possible fruit is re-entering the womb of a mother to receive a new opportunity to fulfill the unfulfilled spiritual achievement.

The fourth fruit is to steal the bodily life of an alive person who has a weak or scattered soul. This type of robbery is the lowest, but it is still a kind of fruit. Its purpose is to have the support of a body in order to continue his cultivation and escape the interruption caused by the death of the previous body. It is traditional knowledge.

The first to the third can be taught. The fourth is your own business. You do it by yourself. It is a situation of exception. It is definitely not my recommendation. This is a serious matter. Who would be the chosen person? Usually the one who makes this choice is an ineffective person who would only choose another sloppy person, thus making no improvement. The kind of body one steals is a serious choice. It is not the best opportunity, though you still maintain the entirety of your conscious being. All healthy life has its own natural protection, so the robber must attack a weak or unprotected person like a new-born baby, a child at a certain age or an adult with a low destiny. This can happen in two different situations. In one situation, if the body is stolen by an achieved one with some degree of achievement, but not yet complete, it would cause the young life to become dumb because the invading soul still has some power to control and express internal disharmony. In the other, if it is stolen by an average soul of some strength or power, the house now has two main souls, and it causes conflict and leads the person to insanity. Usually, insanity has other causes. This is a special situation. When there is a conflict between two main souls in a person, sometimes a strong hatred of the original soul develops in the entering soul. Then the two souls cannot live together any more and they decide to give up the life. There is no benefit to be seen. I do not recommend it.

For your knowledge, I have done this service.

Q: Please elucidate on the first three methods of this cultivation and how to do it.

Master Ni: The practice is the same. The achievement as the good harvest or good fruit is on three levels as I have mentioned. As to how to achieve it, the practice is what I always recommend: to nurture your spirit until it can be independent once the body fails. That is not the main spiritual goal of our spiritual cultivation; it is continual spiritual evolution after having made all efforts to cultivate yourself. The fruit is bore from your spiritual cultivation, as I discussed in various books of my work without labeling or calling it as such. This is the book which discusses it the most.

Chapter 4

Reaching Your Living Soul

Q: Master Ni, please tell us about the function of the human soul of a person who is alive. Mostly we have heard ghost stories and vague references from other sources. No where else can we obtain true knowledge of the living soul.

Master Ni: Many times you have heard the religious expression of saving the soul. It is the essential practice, attraction or key point of religious service. However, the services given by the general level of religions have not provided any real effect or benefit for a soul when it completely withdraws from the world at the end of his physical life. Death is a natural end of physical life. There are also unnatural deaths, which are more difficult. Natural or unnatural, death is not something that a person can stop or avoid. Neither can any religion do anything to stop it. Religious services may minister to a superficial psychological consolation, but offer no real, lasting effect to help the evolution of a soul or to help it move through the transition of death. In a natural life, it is more important to reach each your own soul when you are alive in order to bring fullness to your life, instead of negatively hoping that your soul will be saved after you die. Thus, reaching one's own soul is the focus of the practice of original Taoism. Have you heard the proverb that says, "A kind hearted person to whom you can go for help is better than the God who lives in Heaven?" This proverb exists because an alive person can be the union of God and a flesh form. A God is only an unformed life.

In the real sphere, people do have souls. A soul itself is energy; it is spiritual energy. A soul can be lost or confused. When born into a shape of life and especially when making a sudden change from one stage of life to a different world, stage or range, a soul can suffer.

During the process from birth to death, the average person does not notice that he has a soul. He does notice that he has dreams. In dreams, he sees different people, but surely it is not a matter of people coming into his mind. Often modern people treat their dreams as a kind of residue of the images deeply impressed by their daily life experience. That is true too; that is on one level.

At midnight, if you relax to the fullest possible degree, you go into a trance; your sleep becomes deep. Then your soul starts to become active. It becomes active by one of two possible ways. The first way it becomes active is by light dreaming. This happens if you live a harmonized life. In that case, usually your dreams are light: nothing too troublesome. The second way the soul becomes active is through vivid or troubled dreams. This happens for people who have physical trouble or life trouble. In that case, usually one's dreams are not caused by one's nervousness out of sensory reaction to stimulation by the world. One's dreams are the tension of one's own soul by which a play is created on a stage by the interpretation of the weak mind. The center of the mind is in sleep. The message is expressed as a dream or a show as a report to the center of the mind or you, because the body spirits do not use the way of language to communicate with you. I mean, dreams or pictures are used as a means of communication, rather than language. They like to show you, to give a hint to your mind of whatever important or unresolved thing they feel is important. However, unfortunately most people do not know how to use the information from their dreams to adjust their psychological attitudes towards the important situation, or to help them straighten out the problem.

So what we understand from the matter of dreaming is that the soul and the mind are two separate yet linked systems. Usually both sides work well for the person who is spiritually achieved. His mind supplements the limitations of the spiritual information. Also, the spiritual entities in him help supplement the natural limitations of the function of mind. That is beautiful; it is a kind of teamwork.

However, there is still one natural fact above all of those levels of reality. Even a spiritually developed person, in some circumstances, cannot avoid the natural cycle of changes. What must happen, will happen. In such inalterable situations, a person can only make psychological changes to cope with the events, such as to have more patience and exercise more tolerance towards whatever happens. Therefore, the achievements from learning how to use the teamwork of the mind and spirit do not change a person's fortune, though it does affect one's destiny by moderating the extremes. The level of harmonizing mind and spirit is a basic achievement. It is, at least, attaining internal harmony between the soul and the mind.

You might say to me that even internal harmony does not make things perfect for you, because you still have external limitations. It is true; all people have some limitations in the human realm. This is how the achieved sages can still be fooled by people with a cunning mind who bring about external difficulties. It is not a normal for people to have cunning minds. A normal situation is one in which people are honest and earnest, and such a situation is perfect, as I see it, even though there may still be external limitations. By living a natural, honest life, everything is much easier for the spirit, body and mind. It is perfection because no more complication is brought about than one's soul can help, or that a person can handle. A person may still be considered as a loser in the judgmental eyes of the world. However, just because one does not appear externally as a winner does not mean he is suffering.

If a person has not achieved this type of internal harmony that allows him to live a natural, honest life, perhaps his soul can be of some help, but his mind cannot help because his overly strong desires affect his spiritual clarity. Or perhaps there is another influence through the mind that makes the person unable to escape the problem.

Sages do many things that can be considered as examples for working towards a good world. But some of them are unable to take advantage of their spiritual achievement in handling their own fortune, and perhaps things do not go as smoothly in that area.

There are many people who are achieved. However, most of them do not let anyone know of their achievement.

There are two kinds of true knowledge in life. I am excluding talking about intellectual knowledge, because it is different. One kind of knowledge is spiritual knowledge. This can be exemplified by a person whose life goes fairly smoothly and who encounters no great difficulty or trouble. There is nothing awkward that happens to him. Why do things go all right for him? No one can see it, but the person's internal spiritual system is so strong that he can manage all the things that arise in his life, and he can resolve all the trouble beforehand or at the right circumstance. This is one kind of knowledge that cannot be described much. High, nonverbal knowledge cannot be told or described.

The second kind of knowledge is what we learn through our experience in the world. We learn hot from fire, cold from water and sting from thorny plants. We need to experience vividly, pain! hot! cold! Often experience is the only teacher for many people; that is okay, except when people get stuck in only learning from bad, painful or negative experiences. Many lives create so many stories of negative experience because they have not yet quieted down their lives enough and therefore their souls cannot help. When the soul is not related with the mind, it cannot communicate with the mind and therefore it cannot impart its wisdom. Although every person has a mind, if the mind is blind and not developed, it will not serve a person well. In certain people, the soul cannot reach or communicate with the mind, because in their head, there are so many walls built.

Q: Walls?

Master Ni: Yes, I am not talking about physical walls, like in a building, but about energy walls that block a person's vision. Even in an individual self, there are lots of walls. Nobody can really change any other person unless this individual knows how to break down the walls within himself first. This is why when I take a student, I do not have the authority or power to change him. I can only offer my teaching; unless the person himself breaks down the walls one by one to let in the spiritual air and light, nothing will happen. Spiritual growth and learning is a self-accomplished job.

All of this is important; however, my purpose in giving this talk is to discuss a real practice or method about how an individual can attain a soul party. A party is a friendly gathering of individuals who come together to enjoy themselves. In human life, it may be a bridge party, a chess party or any type of social party. Parties can be good and healthy, or they can be unhealthy. The practice that I am introducing is a particular practice that is exclusive to each individual. No one knows that he has a soul unless this method is learned and used. In this practice, which I call the soul party, a person will experience the reality that his individual soul is a group of souls, and that they can leave one's body. One's main soul and mind will remain in the body, and the other souls will join you for a nice meal. This reality can be experienced by a person. The many soul partners are with each person for a long time as they go through life together, however, few people know them.

Do you see partners inside of you? Once a person regularly follows a general practice for spiritual growth like those in the *Workbook for Spiritual Development*, and once a person has sufficient knowledge from all my other books, especially the *Tao Teh Ching*, he will be prepared for the safety of this soul party.

When I was a student, I learned this practice, but I also know this truth; I do not need to split the soul unity. The good teaching, which is the highest teaching of Lao Tzu, is that a person always needs to maintain oneself in a good spiritual whole. A person remains healthy when he remains in one piece, unified. But for the purpose of teaching, it can be beneficial to experience a soul party one time. It will help a person to know that he indeed has a party of souls who accompany him.

I have been a teacher for a long time, but for the most part I have not taught much, but now I feel I must release my special knowledge obtained from that practice and others. In this time, people have become more objective about spiritual knowledge in a good way. People have more skepticism about the spiritual truth and they also have skepticism about

modern science; they might look at each in a balanced way.
Spiritual reality is natural truth. It cannot be described,
programmed or shaped by any religion. Maybe the religions
can be some level of expression of spiritual reality, but they
are not spiritual reality itself. They are only an accurate or
inaccurate description of spiritual reality.

The first thing in doing any important spiritual cultivation which benefits your soul is to choose a good energy day,
like, for example, the vernal equinox which occurs on March
20 or 21; the summer solstice which is on either June 21 or
22; the autumnal equinox, on September 23 or 24; or the
winter solstice, on December 22 or 23. To find out the exact
hour of the celestial event, one can call a public radio station,
local astronomical observatory, weather station or any place
related with this type of service. The exact hour is different
each year. If it is not convenient to do it on one of those days,
or if a person does not have a way to find out the hour, then
any good day and time will do. It must, however, be a fine
day that is not stormy. Any mild, calm day will be a good day
to use for that purpose.

Before I give you the practical procedure of this soul
party, I need to tell what you will feel or experience. It is
important for a person to understand what he will feel when
he does the method. Otherwise a person might miss it,
because it is so subtle. For those students who are developing themselves, at the beginning they do not know how big
their soul is, because they do not see or notice it.

My personal experience at the beginning of my own soul
party was immediately to feel something internally, from the
high level, sink down. In other words, internally, something
that feels like many pieces of tiny particles which are the
internal spirits transforming in a way that responds to me,
sinks down into the soles of the feet. I call those tiny pieces
spiritual particles. When the spirits stay inside, you do not
know them, because there is no sensory feeling that can be
associated with them. Once they reach your outer, sensible
part, you shall know of their existence because you can feel
them like a gentle touch.

When a person does a soul party, it is better not to tell
anyone about it. I went out to have my soul party in a small

restaurant, although usually it is preferable to do it in a quiet, solitary place. But the restaurant was the only appropriate place available to me at the time, so I went in and sat down at a table where I could be alone. When I picked up the menu, I noticed an immediate response from the group of souls. I felt their presence, and noticed that they wanted to choose what to eat. As I looked at the menu, it was clearly not a matter of myself ordering whatever I wanted. I immediately felt interference - I wonder that interference is the right word - but the interference was simple. When I went to choose something, immediately I knew whether it was right or wrong. At that time, because I was much younger, I liked to eat food that was a bit spicy; but no, I could tell immediately that they disapproved of that choice. Or if I wished to select something too sweet; no, it was prohibited. They had better knowledge about food than I did at that time. So by confirming or disapproving what I was going to select, they chose the food. When what I choose was agreeable, I felt a general feeling of all right; if it was not a suitable dish, I felt different sensations, like there was an objection.

Then what happened? I felt somebody touch my left shoulder. It felt like somebody was sitting invisibly at my side; and on the right side, gently patting me, was someone else. Because I could not see them, and my experience was in a public restaurant, I did not know how many were in front of me, sitting at the table. I did not know if there were enough seats for all of them. I ordered only enough food for one person; actually, just a little more than that. That was my experience.

Q: Were they your internal spirits, the hun and po, or were they the external spirits, who live around us all the time, as you say?

Master Ni: It cannot be truthfully distinguished. However, a normal and healthy life has natural spiritual protection. A person does not need to worry about who joins him, with or without an invitation. Simply, without a doubt, they are a person's life partners.

Q: So after you finished the meal and left the restaurant, did your life always remain that way, or did you have to do something to make things normal again?

Master Ni: You are normal. But your spiritual knowledge of yourself will be increased. In a good way, the assertiveness of a person's intellectual mind can be more opened to responding to signals which might come from one's partners as their knowledge. Usually if there is no signal expressed, it means okay. But for your safety in making decisions, a person would do well to follow his general knowledge or combine it with the understanding received from the signals. Practically, in this stage, signals cannot be defined as right or wrong. This means that the signals are given, but it is up to you to interpret their application to the situation in front of you. This can be remembered if you are ambitious to use the signal of the spirits in making decisions in every day life.

In other words, you are still responsible for your own decisions. The advice from the spirits is only advice, and if you act only according to their suggestions, you may not always be making the appropriate decisions.

Q: Do the souls actually eat the food?

Master Ni: They take energy of the food through you.

Q: Is the soul party the same thing as attaining Tao?

Master Ni: No. It is to discover the reality of oneself. It would be one step of self-understanding. Attaining Tao is opposite; that is to hold the unity. In the minds of some people, if deep understanding is not reached, attaining Tao cannot be understood.

Let us return to the soul party. It is advisable to do it, especially for the purpose of truthful knowledge for oneself and one's friends. My teacher at the time - I was a student of advanced Chinese medicine - said that there is a lot of benefit gained from doing it. Basically, as I understand it, the benefit is in the spiritual level. At least a person truly knows he is not the only lord in his life. A person is not alone trying to do everything by himself. Usually in life, a person feels that he is like a young boss: a person who knows nothing about business, but is in the position of a business authority who needs to manage everything smoothly despite his naivete, inexperience and assertion. Doing the soul party helps one know that help is available.

So I enjoyed the dinner and came back home, and it was fulfilled. It is called soul party.

Whatever you learn from your teachers' books or from the ancient sages' teachings is just a discussion of things of this type. But a person never learns the thing until he decides to do it; then when he has done it, he is experienced. Then, a person knows that he has partners. He knows that it is he who is responsible to slow down a little bit and listen to what the partners wish to tell him.

How does a person slow down and learn to listen to them? One slows down in decision making, for example, by pausing for one night or for several hours, to observe things quietly before making the decision. Do not hurry. A person does not say, "Oh, poor me, I singly need to make this decision to go or do whatever in five minutes." If any person does that, then one or two hours later, he congests up tightly with anxiety, and his silent, invisible partners cannot associate with him.

It does not matter how old a person is, from sixteen to sixty or even older, a person himself can never gain enough world experience to be able to singly make excellent decisions all of the time. A person never has enough world experience, because our human knowledge system is that first we must experience pain in order to know pain. Our silent, invisible partners, on the other hand, do not need to experience something to know about it; they simply know it. They are gods. Each of us is only human, and can benefit from their advice. So on one hand, you admire the different capabilities of the souls in your group, but on the other hand, you still need to rely on the general knowledge you have gathered, the habitual way of doing things and the common way of people. I mean, we admire that the spiritual knowledge capability is direct, but on the other hand, we must use our experience

and common sense to handle our worldly affairs. That is
what we are all about.

The last 3,000 to 5,000 years shows a great development
in written language and intellectual development. The mind
is an important part of our being as humans. But despite
that development, whenever we take bodily form in the world,
we find that some of us do not mature. This is because
maturity is not only physical, nor is it only mental. Maturity
happens when we experience growth in all three areas. If a
person only learns or grows in one area, he will not be
balanced. When we are born into the world, spiritually we are
doing fine, because we are refreshed by coming into the new
life. But most people wear out their souls or spiritual
strength too quickly through seeking sensory pleasures or
social status and keep their mind undeveloped.

*Q: Do you mean that it is a person's spiritual strength that
develops his mind?*

Master Ni: Yes. In the subtle level, the mind is composed of
a group of spirits. They need development to bring about the
development of mind. In other words, if a person puts his
energy out into the world while young instead of into educating himself, the mind may not develop fully. Generally, the
mind has natural tendencies. People may be good at some
things and not at others. Wholeness of mind or a fully
developed mind is precious to an individual and to the world.

My teaching promotes spiritual development in order to
develop the wholeness and the fullness of mind of each
individual. I have just mentioned, most people wear out their
own spiritual strength too quickly before they develop their
mind. That is sad. It is much better and healthier to keep
one's fresh, new life as pure as that of a baby. The soul itself
has a different time cycle than a body. That is also an
interesting point. If you would like to know more about the
time cycle of a soul, you must discover it by yourself through
spiritual development. It is not intellectual experience.

Also, rather than making our mind complicated and
sophisticated, we need to keep our mind in a simple, pure
state. Do we need optimism? Yes. Do we need positive

attitudes? Yes. Do we need caution? Yes. Do we need to be self-managed? Yes. Do most people achieve that? No, they do not. Their mind thinks, "Yes, I can do everything," but they cannot. They try to argue in front of truth. They disobey truth. They accept cultural junk as truth.

There is no way that a person can help other people until he breaks down his own inner walls. Please break down your walls. But that is not the point; I have already more or less taught all of you how to break down the inner walls in my other written works. Sometimes I have translated the sages whose material has helped me, or have given other information when I myself was inspired in different circumstances by my students. My books are not something I plan and create beforehand just to sell. They develop from true life experience, and how the situations of life inspire me and stir my spirit. I wish to catch and accurately relay the messages that come from the highly developed divine soul to me, as this flesh body as Master Ni. It is my sincere wish to pass these messages along to you.

If you do the soul party, you will discover that all the souls in the group know you, and you are the only one who does not know them. You are the one who is the student: a young king or queen who needs more development. You are the one who is responsible for your life boat. So often it seems that there is nowhere you can reach for help. You are also one of the souls with spiritual blockages that have been created by intellectual learning, worldly experience and your own impulses. But now, you are the main rowing hand of the life boat. Where do you take yourself to? If you do not develop yourself and remain open to listening to your spiritual partners, and instead listen to the world's misguidance, you may not end up in a place you would like to be.

II

By reading, learning, experiencing, pondering and cultivating, you are saving the soul, or the soul saves you. This is developing our soul; this is our learning. We need to know the requirements or what we need to do; transform it into your own inner guidance in order to achieve it.

First, the purpose of the practice of the soul party is to supply people with a way to know the natural foundation of individual life in the spiritual aspect and also to develop intellectual knowledge through spiritual experience. So before doing the soul party, a person needs cultivation and needs to conform with the truthful way of living I have described in this and other works.

Second, this kind of practice is suitable for a person who has reached some maturity and is not too young. Young people who read about it should remember that there is such a practice for their personal knowledge, and when they come to the right stage, they can do it. It is not suitable for a person to do it at an age that is too young. A young person's life is not stable, his understanding is not deep enough, and he does not know his own interest. Those things will cause trouble.

Third, people who have any strong conflict in personality should not do it. That will not help them. This describes a person for whom there is no psychological peace as general people experience. Please use my other teachings to help yourself. It is not suitable to be ambitious when one does not yet have personal unity.

Fourth, people who are not in good health or in a stage of being able to control one's own life should not do it. People who fall deeply in love, are suffering from disappointment in love or have a strong emotional disturbance are not in a suitable life condition to have a soul party.

Fifth, if a person wishes to do it and is at the right stage and a mature age, he should first have full knowledge of all kinds of teaching I give before doing the soul party. In that case, he is fully equipped with a general good spiritual understanding, and will know how to handle himself. It is particularly important to understand the introduction, and repeatedly read about what will happen. In that way a person will have a full understanding of the matter.

Sixth, suppose there is some difficulty that happens afterwards out of one's own spiritual discovery. It means that the person has not followed Tao well and is not virtuous enough to give oneself a bright spiritual future. Such a person is going a different way than the way of Tao. In such a case, it is always important to reflect over one's life activities, one's small internal thoughts and harmful old habits. A person must seriously work on improving those things. You are the one who is responsible for your own life being, and you cannot mess around with it.

So if trouble happens, read the *Heavenly Way* over and over again. Then do something like good deeds and give help to people in the right circumstances. I do not mean to create an opportunity, but once the opportunity of a good, healthy situation comes, give some help without asking credit for the service. Only that can help a person dissolve his internal spiritual difficulty. The special term for that is called virtuous fulfillment; it is the most powerful practice in the spiritual world.

The example of the virtuous work of humanistic realization is not limited to one's particular religious background. Any humanistic work can be considered as a good example of virtuous fulfillment. That is just an example; everybody has a chance to do virtuous fulfillment in a different way according to one's background, skills or training. If a person is a president, a politician, a waitress, a shoe shine boy or whatever, he or she always has a chance to give help to people and exercise good influence to bring a positive contribution to others. Virtuous fulfillment is the best rescue of individual destiny. But it is not something that a person can do for one month and then quit if he wishes to achieve himself spiritually.

In my own experience, I was a student of all religions. I have learned their kind spirits, how they give service, their good motivations, and how they have a good heart. I do not take their foolish structure. In each religion, there are always people who are highly achieved spiritually. In any of the different religious backgrounds, there are people who are less conceptual, who work for the reality of their own individual person and who use the religious formality to improve themselves and extend their service to the world.

Seven, do not use any worldly conception to mix up or confuse yourself; just enjoy the natural reality. In other words, enjoy the experience and do not try to analyze it meticulously, because you cannot. The purpose of this exercise is to increase one's knowledge of this level. But if a person wants true spiritual achievement and development, he needs to work thoroughly for spiritual learning.

Eight, this practice provides a foundation of knowledge which can more or less help a person's development. It will not save a person time or energy in his cultivation. Nor will it avoid anything that needs to be fulfilled. Most people are looking for an immortal pill that they just swallow so they do not need to do any work or improve their personality. The immortal pill is the sun in the sky; we are supported by its shining. We are all active and receive the sun's benefit through our work each day, and thus move towards immortality, gradually and safely.

There is no immortality pill that a person can eat once and become achieved. Nor is there a one-time exercise that can be done and then a person is achieved. Spiritual growth is a process that occurs over time. The soul party is just a start. It provides a person with the knowledge of what life is, spiritually.

If a person truly understands that spiritual growth is a process and is willing to work for it, then doing the soul party will be safe for him to do, because it is the reality of life. It is what you are; there is nothing to add to it and nothing to decrease. Many books and sages teach many things, but nobody teaches what a person is composed of spiritually. All the books are only descriptions. Now we come to a different level, which is that of experience.

I wish that my beloved students who are serious, hard-working, stable, mature and dedicated, would learn it. Be serious as a student of life and of yourself. Your own life is a path; it is a religion of development.

But be certain that you meet the correct conditions before you do it. That is my warning. In this part, I will explain about the practice so that if you wish, and if you feel ready for it, you may be able to learn it from your teacher and make your own new self discovery.

III

It is the teaching of the ancient developed one: the master of human life is one's own spiritual energy and physical essence. If spiritual energy and physical energy or essence come together, they will guide one to reach the truth. A person can discover the spiritual reality of oneself and nature. Those who do not know how to nurture their spiritual energy and how to nurture their physical essence will receive no response from their prayers.

So the foundation of nurturing or cultivating one's spiritual and physical energy should be learned. Several other suitable days for the soul party are the second day of the new moon or the second day of the full moon of each month.

In the month before a person does this practice of soul party, it is important that he meditate at least five times. I am talking about correct meditation, which is quiet sitting that is not stiff or rigid. It is important to give oneself time to be alone and be quiet. Generally, people are too busy to do that; but five times is the minimum requirement. Meditating for a short while every day, all year round, is of course ideal. After you have a good preparation your spiritual sensitivity is sharp and strong.

I hope all of you will use it correctly to know the reality of life. Then you will view life differently, take care of your life differently, organize yourself differently and live a good life. If you wish to help yourself and people, all my teachings will support your new experience.

Q: Is this practice what is called opening the bottle?

Master Ni: This is not as risky as opening the bottle or gourd of one's life being. It is the spiritual communication of one's own spirits. If everything is normal, the result is positive.

Q: What is a suitable age to do this soul party? You mentioned that it is better for a person to be mature, and we know that different people mature at different times, but what about an average person.

Master Ni: When a person is young, he is too emotional. He cannot manage himself well. He is not mature. Older people also have emotion, but they have more experience in knowing how to handle it. So mature means perhaps middle age. Generally speaking, doing the soul party after age sixty will be safe. It depends on the individual. However, I believe that after sixty is safe.

If you are a scientist, you have a purpose of improving human knowledge in modern time. You might like to extend yourself to a little bit of spiritual experience. I believe that you will be the one to become the bridge between ancient and modern development, especially when you do a great job to open up the blockage of modern knowledge of spiritual reality.

For a general spiritual student, I believe it is sufficient just to read it and know about channeling your spiritual energy. You do not have to do it. The effect is still the same; the benefit a person receives is the same. This does not contradict what I said earlier that you do not know it until you experience it. By learning it from another's experience, you shall have the benefit without the disbenefit of suddenly discovering that you are faced with so many partners. This is why I give the warning. It is a person's own responsibility. If you hurry to do it without having any good purpose, then you might need to take long to put yourself together.

Scientists should do it, because they need to break through to bring the truth to people. For general people or spiritual students, this is one of the selective spiritual practices. There are many ways one can reach it. It only gives a basic foundation of human people, it is not the high spiritual achievement. For spiritual achievement, a person needs to read about and conform oneself with the truth and wisdom given by the ancient sages.

Q: My inner feeling is that a person will know when he is ready. If you have any doubt whether you are ready, then do not do it. You will know, from a deep inner feeling, when to do it.

Master Ni: It is not a matter of doubt or no doubt. It is matter of seriousness in spiritual pursuit. It is an intellectual attitude that says, "I need to know my life." The goal of a serious student is the satisfaction of his intellectual mind to know the truth of spiritual reality. It is one side of general intellectual knowledge. A person may know many things, but still make no spiritual progress. The practice of soul party is of a different nature. It can bring a person to a new range of life.

Spiritual achievement is your own work. I recommend, I teach and I give examples, but it still depends on you. What matters is if you are open to it, how deeply you are involved with it and how much you would like to bring that as the true path of your life. Once you learn the practices, the benefit is yours. All spiritual knowledge, once published, is for your benefit. This knowledge belongs to society, but how people use it is up to them.

I have made a clear statement here, that one's spiritual growth and doing this practice is one's own spiritual responsibility. Saving the soul is not a matter of believing in God. Saving a soul is a matter of your virtuous being. If you are virtuous, you are God, or the soul has saved you from deep downfall. There is no exception for anyone.

Myself, I do not consider that I have much spiritual learning or have accomplished much personal spiritual merit through healing people for a charge, writing books or helping people reach their own spiritual reality. I still do not think I have done virtuous fulfillment. I am naturally welcoming whatever bigger, harder job is ahead waiting for me. Was it not the great Mo Tzu whose life made a great example that "the worth of life is to do what benefits all people and not to do what is harmful to all people?" For the benefit of the world, I will make no excuse. I teach all the important secrets to the right student, not according to their ambition, but according to how hard he works to improve himself and his attitudes, and especially his realization of virtuous fulfillment. This is a traditional standard that is required from a student learning from the model of Mo Tzu, though we could not be exactly what he has been. At least his spirit pointed out a direction in which a Taoist should go. This practice of the soul party was handed down by him and can be traced back to the Great Yu. The general guidance of this great sage has been absorbed by the students of Chuang Tzu in the learning of Tao to balance their spiritual self-cultivation and worldly service. A complete life is the realization of internally and externally balanced fulfillment. The truth of life is demonstrated by such a one.

If a person trusts it, this practice will be beneficial. The spirits will be able to communicate to the person better, and they will tell him in advance about big things that will happen, such as when it is his time to leave this world.

By doing this practice, a person will be able to prove the existence of his soul. This beneficial practice has been passed down from unnamed spiritually developed ones, through the sages and the Great Yu to us.

So, one day your voyage will be accomplished. You will land on the shore of immortality, and no longer stay in the boat. Nobody can physically stay alive forever. The body follows a different law, like the nature of trees. But a person's uncontaminated soul can be kept fresh and new, unburdened by worldly memories and troubles, etc.

There is no lasting value to worldly experience except building up your spiritual durability. If something was happy, it has passed; if it was painful, it has also passed. The soul itself is much more valuable than the transient experiences of the world, in which happiness and pain come and go.

At least, if a person practices the soul party technique, he will sustain his natural vitality, and shall at least reform himself to come back in the right circumstance. His soul is saved. He can reach for the second or the first fruit. The first kind of fruit is for the ones who are more serious and have learned the higher practice about the fruit. See the section about the four fruits of spiritual achievement for further understanding in the previous chapter.

Chapter 5

Life Force Comes From Inside

Before I came to the United States, a man named Mr. Koo, Yun-che came to me in China looking for to learn the spiritual practices of my tradition. He became a student before I moved to the United States. He is the only overseas Chinese I know in the United States, because my new direction is to work helping my western friends. My teaching in China is totally different than here. Here it is mostly spiritual guidance. I have not taught the traditional practices too much yet. However, in China there is a practical need to relate life and death with spiritual development.

Mr. Koo had good confidence. Just last year, when he was in his 70s, he spiritually knew he needed to choose how to go away. His body was in good shape and he had lots of money. He had been the owner of a big textile factory in China. He periodically went to Las Vegas to play the card games. He did that just to pass time, because he was not seriously expecting to win.

Last year, he started cultivating himself seriously. His nature at that time was to stop all eating. He did not need to eat anything, so for six months he ate nothing. By doing that, he cleaned himself up. He had his two sons bring him to me to confirm the final instruction of ascending. I repeated to him that if the soul exits out the top of the head, it will ascend to heaven. But if the soul goes through the lower part, it is bad. So he knew that the matter was important.

Just before he passed, he called his sons over and told them clearly what should be done in their lives. Then he told them everything about what he attained and proved and said that those were his final words to his family. On that night, he went away, spiritually. After that, the body stayed in his bed for seven days. He looked asleep and in good health, and there was no bad odor. His family thought he was just in a good meditation. They were just waiting for him to wake up, despite their father having told them everything as his last words. All of them thought he was still alive, and nobody was scared. They called me up on the telephone to seek my instruction about what they could do to see if he was still there or not. I told them to use something that would make a soft bell-like noise, such as a certain type of Chinese instrument or tapping a rice bowl with a spoon, and strike it by each ear. If the soul was inside the body, the response would be to wake up.

Because there was no response, they realized that he had passed. Then they noticed that at the top of his head, there was an opening where the bone had parted and the soul had exited. That opening could be seen, even by his sons, because it was physical. The sons were happy for his true achievement.

He is achieved respectfully. He is the only student who proved this in the United States. I have seen many in China. So the soul is more important than the physical body. The soul decides to stay or go, and he achieved beautifully. Mr. Koo was a rich person who suffered under Communism, but he did not care about the loss of money. He took his sons to Brazil, then came to the United States. He stayed in Monterey Park and enjoyed the same Chinese way of life. He only did serious cultivation in his last few years, yet he did so well. Before he passed away, he had hemorrhoids and other small problems here and there. Through his serious cultivation, he overcame all the problems. There was no kind of sickness anymore through his spiritual practice. It was his decision to go, nobody influenced him. He thought it was time with his spiritual clarity and achievement. But it is not death, it is a kind of new life in a higher way.

Mr. Koo's sons seemed to learn something by observing their father's process. They were not sad. They were happy about their father educating them about Taoism and proving it to them. The father made a good example, he could stay and go by his free will. That is interesting.

I truly believe that if a person decides to manage his own life, usually he has enough energy to do it. Once you hire lots of undeveloped people to take care of your life, it is usually not as good as taking care of yourself.

Chapter 6

Saving Your Soul

Student A: Is there any truth at all to the idea of saving the soul? After all, so many religions talk about it. And from what danger is a person's soul supposed to be saved?

Student B: Master Ni, we have heard a lot about the religious teachings of saving the soul. It is said that following a certain religion or religious leader will save a person. But is there a real practice of saving one's soul? It seems to me that there is always a deeper, more truthful understanding behind the shallow level of religious practice, that I am not aware of until someone explains it to me.

Also, from what is the soul being saved?

Master Ni: In my recent work, I use the conventional conception of saving the soul as the topic of my talks. I believe these talks, which are included in several of my recent books, give a pretty good understanding of the matter of saving the soul. My usual approach is to share the deep reality of a subject. My subject now is still the soul. Each life has its soul. The soul is the essence of a life. Souls develop distinctively depending on the type of life and what stage it is in. Dissimilar kinds of life have different kinds of souls. Also, in the various stages of an individual human life, the soul will change as it evolves or devolves.

On the animal level, once the shape or bodily form is destroyed, the essence cannot be kept. It scatters or flies to attach to something else. No deep sense of identity is developed, so animals can only be considered as a different level of natural energy. What makes human life so important is its internal development which evolves from a complete foundation of five elements.

Generally speaking, a human individual has a soul. The soul is the internal being of an individual. Let's use this understanding to go further. Let us take, for example, a kind-hearted person who always contributes and is involved with all kinds of charitable work in addition to living a healthy life.

Is this person's soul beautiful? Yes, she is internally beautiful, doubtlessly, so the person enjoys respect and love from others. Such goodness comes to her life because of her work to constantly improve herself and the world; thus, the person possesses a beautiful soul.

Now let us look at some criminals. There are different types of criminals: some are circumstantial criminals and some are deep-rooted criminals. They are different types of people. A circumstantial criminal meets trouble in life because he cannot control his life or the events in it, so a mistake is made. The circumstances make the person do wrong. The spirits of that type of person have no deep involvement with criminal behavior.

Now let us talk about deep rooted criminals. Do they have a soul? Yes, they have a soul. Then why are they so bad? It is because of their level of internal development. They are not evolved enough to have self respect, and their sense of self-interest has been distorted or exaggerated. Surely when a person establishes his own individuality, personal interest is involved. But once a person satisfies his own individual needs to some extent, he will usually no longer continue to try to bring the wealth of the entire world into his pocket. Deep criminals have their own theory about why they acted the way they did; they do not talk about things like being lazy or not following a decent life path. Instead, they always complain about the world. They do not take responsibility for their own failure in being able to support themselves financially, or satisfaction in their life, and therefore they turn out to be a criminal. Criminals can have emotional, psychological, immoral or satanic energy but their spiritual light is dimmed or extinguished by what they do.

We have already mentioned that the kind-hearted person has a soul that enjoys respect and warmth from people. The cruel criminal also has a soul, but his soul receives a different treatment, mostly from himself. In ancient times, when the authorities of society decided to punish a criminal, the retribution was bodily suffering, such as beating, being chained, removing a bodily part or execution. Is the soul punished? It seems they punished the body instead of punishing the soul. But the real criminal is not the body; the real criminal is the distorted or mixed up soul inside the body. Even after the body-house is finished, whether it be a kind-hearted person or a criminal, the soul still survives. This is something really worth looking into for one's personal understanding of the nature of life. An individual human life is an interesting composition. Usually people think there is one single soul in each person. Yes, there is a main soul, but there is also a group of spirits, called a group soul. In order not to confuse them, we will talk about the main soul as "soul" and the other souls as "spirits." All are organized into an individual. The spirits can be produced by the body or attracted by the person's spiritual or mental quality and practice. One's quality of practice issues a vibration which attracts the corresponding energies. This means, a person creates his being and personal reality through his firstly private thoughts and ideas. His being radiates with the thoughts he thinks, and a certain vibration resonates which attracts corresponding or similar energies. Those energies manifest as his friends and environment. This gives new understanding to the well-known proverb, "Birds of a feather flock together;" it means, a person will feel most comfortable around energies that are similar to his own. In other words, when a person thinks good thoughts, he does good and good people and good things come into his life.

There are some schools of thought that believe that most people are born about the same, and that the environment determines their personalities. That would mean that a good environment would create a good person and a bad environment would create a bad person. However, that is not always the case. A person is totally responsible for his nature and for the quality of his life. Thus, sometimes when a person is born into a good family or society, he can still have bad tendencies. Also, some people who are born into bad circumstances or grow in a bad environment, can be as gentle, fresh and beautiful as a lotus flower. We see that the theory of environmental determination does not always reflect the apparent reality.

Truthfully, the evolution of an individual's soul determines his personality. When a main soul receives a new shape of life, the person is given an opportunity to learn spiritually, and to grow and nurture high inner spirits. These inner spirits rely on the main soul for their guidance or direction in life. You are the main soul. You are the teacher; you are the boss, the leader, the god or devil head. First, you affect the lower level of your spirits. Second, by your vibration or radiation, you can attract bad energy or bad spirits to come and join your life. They might make your hand do irresponsible things and make your body take responsibility for those things. A deep rooted criminal, for example, would do the evil things until he eventually loses his life opportunity by capital punishment.

We have already discussed how people do wrong things and cause trouble for themselves. In another type of situation, people make mistakes and then suffer punishment by losing profit or important opportunities. Such a mistake could be caused by confusion created by one's spiritual enemies. The spiritual enemies make sabotaging suggestions to the mind of a person; the invasion of the enemy spirit manifests as confusion or confused thinking.

For example, if a person did wrong in his past lives such as killing or harming people, in his new life opportunity, things may happen which have no apparent cause. The person who was previously wronged may still remain in shadow or ghost form and follow the wrongdoer to the present life. The wrongdoer receives the confusion or thought-suggestion to do wrong from the enemy spirit.

Also, if in a present life, a person kills or harms people or does some evil, although he may still hold thoughts of self importance, he has already damaged his spiritual dignity. Then, any spirits who were the victims will find a chance to take revenge according to the amount of damage caused.

Each individual has natural protection. Each individual knows to protect himself; this is a natural instinct. Even deeply rooted criminals do not like trouble any more than everybody else. They like to make trouble for others, but they do not like trouble for themselves. Why do they make trouble for others and for their own lives? Sometimes, in a low cycle or after drinking, taking drugs, having sex or washing the hair, even if they do not wish to realize their bad motivation, there is an opportunity for other spirits of bad intent to enter their body and confuse them or encourage them to make a wrong decision. This can be costly to their lives. This happens not only on the level of deeply rooted criminals, but also on the level of most people making less important mistakes.

Let us talk about the good side, too. If a person does many favors or good deeds to help people, their ghosts or spirits like to help him. Even a person who is not smart or intelligent, skilled in investments or other things, may find that for no apparent reason his decisions turn out well, he receives unexpected promotions or his actions have good results. One's natural cycle helps a person, but one is also helped by past lives, this life and one's personal spiritual behavior and contacts. Thus, each individual must watch his own contacts and behavior.

Each decision, action and thought affect a person on the level of spirit. Even small details can cause emotional difficulties such as resentment, hatred or hostility. Emotions take a long time to dissolve, so whether you stir up your own or someone else's emotions, some time later, you need to restore the balance or correct your fault. Also, sometimes, you receive help, without noticeable reason.

Religiously, people talk about saving the soul. Which soul is going to be saved? Even if a deep-rooted criminal is killed, his soul continues to live. A soul cannot be killed by a rifle or knife. So it is not a matter of saving the soul, it is a matter of needing a different understanding. Rather than waiting around for someone else to save our soul, we need to directly improve our own life being and conscious being. We improve our life being by improving our understanding of things. We need a different understanding so we can do differently about saving our soul. Saving the soul does not mean to rely on the external forceful image of God. Saving your own soul means to develop your own internal awareness. Conventional religions make soul saving the main preparation for death. It is not. Saving your own soul means to have a good preparation for living a good and righteous life during different stages of personal spiritual awareness.

In fact, when a soul is shaped with flesh, it is like a new marriage between a soul and a body who come together. A union is made. A life that has a body and soul is the center of nature. The soul is like a seed inside a piece of fruit. The body is the fruit around the seed which provides nourishment for its later germination. The seed may have the opportunity to be kept safely by the soil until the spring, when it can sprout and find new life again. Therefore, one knows the importance of natural life with spiritual development. The soul and the body cannot be separated from each other. That is normalcy. Normalcy, or naturalness, is the center of any good life, and is carefully tended as the nourishment for durable life. The goal of a life being is not to be a saved soul after death.

Once a person leaves the body, he looses all ability to create unless he rides on somebody; for example, a strong ghost might travel around and confuse someone who is weak or has problems. Spirits are different from the soul. A group of spirits can work together to confuse or help the mind of a generally healthy person because they are natural essence without identity. A soul, after leaving the body, mostly loses the natural vitality until the next opportunity to incarnate.

Religion attempts to discipline living people by setting up a spiritual standard to have real good affect over the soul of deceased people. It does this through creating a belief structure for people. At one level, that can help people, but ultimately, belief is only psychology: an issue of the mind, not the reality of life. What is important is the kind of life a person lives. That is more truthful than what he believes.

It is a great opportunity for a soul to be reshaped with flesh. It is an opportunity for new life. A person becomes a leader, boss, lord or manager of a group of spirits in his life. It is not assured that in the new life experience one will do really well as a decision-maker in channelling all of one's personal spiritual energy so that it is not wasted or abused and so that no actions will cause a present or future burden. For example, if a soul is shaped with flesh again, the success of the new life depends on its behavior, and its ability to gather life energy. The flesh shape taken by a soul is deter-mined by its past life experiences: behavior, lifestyle and the ability to gather life energy. If a person does something well in a past life, he will have at least three lifetimes in which to enjoy the benefit of what he has achieved. If he does a bad deed, he will have at least three lifetimes in which to suffer for the problem caused.

Saving the soul in conventional thought means that through one's connection with a powerful spiritual God, one will be saved from being thrown into a fire at the time of final judgement. This is totally a religious promotion and is not spiritual reality. The spiritual reality is that you are responsible for yourself. You punish or reward yourself. Life is a continual process of thoughts, decisions and actions.

Among the fruit trees bearing one type of fruit, there are different species. Better seeds can do better. Inferior seeds cannot grow good fruit; it is a waste of time to try to grow them. Human life is not only a matter of improving the fruit, or life, it is a matter of improving the seed, or soul, also. We improve the external life and the internal soul. In actuality, there is no separation between the two parts, the internal and external, although we discuss them that way. The internal and external parts of a human life are not two, but one thing.

This discussion has given a limited representation of the soul. Sometimes when I talk about the soul, I mention one important concept: it is not you who saves the soul, it is the soul that saves you. General religions always talk about saving the soul; they are afraid a soul will be lost if a person does not have faith in some huge, powerful spiritual being outside of himself. This is a stage that a person needs to pass through as he moves on to deeper spiritual reality.

In spiritual cultivation, a person makes the scope of life activity much smaller. With such an opportunity, once a student develops enough, he is taught by his own high soul and high spirits. A beginning student who does not have spiritual experience only experiences his mind. His mind is, however, only organized by the content of his worldly collection of experience. A person may be informative or informed, but may just be repeating what was read or discussed, rather than his own experience.

The main soul is also sometimes called the high soul, higher self or personal god if achieved through many lifetimes of cultivation. In general, there are three voices inside of all people: high voice, middle voice and lower voice. The high voice is the soul; even with high achievement, it still contains the potential of higher evolution. The middle voice is the mind. It listens to all voices and also repeats what was heard from them. The low voice is the body. If you follow the high voice, you move upward. If you follow the lower voice, you move downward. Thus, in general, the educator of a healthy and effective mind holds great importance. How can some people be so successful? Because those people nicely, splendidly, put all opportunities together, even the small ones, to make an enjoyable life. Whether or not a person can enjoy life or not still depends on the wisdom of the mind, which rules your life through creative or destructive decisions.

Sometimes a person's high material achievement makes his middle spirits become proud, and no longer will they listen to the high spirits. They only listen to the low voices that say, "enjoy more, enjoy more"; then all the good achievement that he has brought together turns out to be poison. It becomes a tomb to bury him. This is important for all of us to know so we can be careful about it!

So the general conception of saving the soul is not a reality. Sometimes if a person's life is spiritually centered, the high spirits will not only help with his spiritual evolution but also his material well-being. With the proper focus, everything that comes into a person's life can be something that is like spiritual or material gold which serves him. But once he obtains it, how he uses it and how he enjoys it is another wisdom, another type of development.

It is important that each person have self-respect. It is dangerous to lose one's self-respect. A person, if he occasionally loses his self-respect, needs immediately to restore it, because without it, he may lose his knowledge. The knowledge is this: when a person has received life, he has received a great opportunity. A new opportunity is given to him to alter, change and restore the well being of his soul. He must not fall into the habit of losing self-respect.

Having self respect does not mean that a person has a high position like some authoritative professions. Self respect means he respects his own spirits. I need specifically to point this out because people sometimes misunderstand. It is respecting one's own spirits that gives people godliness. Men are gods and women are goddesses. I do not like gender discrimination; so I will simply say that all people are God if they keep their self respect. If a person loses his self respect, then he is harming himself, his life, somebody else or the world. We do not talk a lot about saving the soul; sometimes a person must let his soul save him by listening to its good advice. Much of the time modern people are too materialistic and affected externally, both of which pulls our focus away from our spiritual center.

I have taught a technique in which I used the conventional term, saving the soul. What is the reality of that? The reality is that people's lives can be either materially centered, sexually centered, emotionally centered or intellectually centered; this is all superficial, not deep. So touching a certain point on the forehead, also called opening the spiritual channel or opening the mystical pass is, to performed to help you restore your head as the spiritual center of the body. The reality of saving the soul is re-channeling one's spiritual energy, putting one's spirit back onto the right path. It is an effective, useful and helpful practice.

Each person is born as a beloved child of nature. I am not establishing myself as the savior of your soul. I am not asking you to pray to me. That is of no use. Pray in your own name, and help yourself. Save your soul by rechanneling and uplifting it. I would like to repeat that to emphasize it: the reality of saving the soul is uplifting and rechanneling one's own soul in the right spiritual channel, and not letting it be confused with the other channels of emotion, sex, material goods, intellect and worldly scatteredness. My personal wish is that all of you blossom fully in spiritual, material and mental realms into having a decent, complete, good life.

Now I would like to discuss more about saving the soul. In this level, I will reveal the traditional effective secret of how to save one's own soul before the end of this chapter. Practically, it is how to enhance the soul of each individual person. First, you might like to know, there are two kinds of theories about saving the soul. I will group them to make them more understandable. One type of theory is that the world will soon end in a tremendous destruction, and that each person's soul needs to be saved. In modern terms, that describes a vast destruction of the entire living environment for human people. It is one method, sorry to point out, that general religion uses to group people. No, I do not need to tell the intention, but they use that theory to make people follow them. They teach that the big destruction will happen soon, and that all people will lose their lives unless they join their group and accept the beliefs they organized. That is one kind of theory of saving the soul.

I will give you the other type of theory of saving the soul. It comes from old Chinese religious beliefs. In the origin of heaven and earth, there were a number of original energy seeds that were sent from heaven down to earth so that they could integrate with earthly energy. Gradually, these seeds developed into souls. They developed as human lives. Those souls, living an earthly life for generation after generation, lifetime after lifetime, began to miss their original heavenly home. Therefore, they used a special practice called saving the soul, which made the souls remember not to be too attached to the worldly game. The practice made them remember where they came from, and to be sure to go back to the heavenly home.

Those soul seeds were originally nurtured in the womb of the mother of the universe. Once they became mature, they descended to earth and split themselves. Some of them still contain the original energy, original chi or original spirit of the heavenly home. Some have already drowned, as in water, by the danger of losing themselves in the world. These need the original connection restored to them, as part of the spiritual vitality of each individual person. That is the second theory about saving the soul.

This is my personal impression. Surely, I welcome any good theory that benefits human people. The first theory about the great destruction of the soul is that only the one who believes in God will be saved. I believe this theory comes from people's fear. They are born in the world with bare hands, no sharp claws, no sharp teeth, no horns on their head. Sometimes, especially in ancient times, people had fear about how to survive in such a rough world. They needed something to give them a feeling of security and encourage them to live in the world. So the fellowship of that kind of religion or path of saving the soul mostly has a foundation of internal insecurity.

Some ancient Taoists established the second theory of the soul. Usually people, and especially modern people, imagine that our ancestors were primitive people who did not know anything and could not even make a fire. But those people are not aware of the conquering power that overcomes all kinds of difficulties. Our ancestors had the ability to use that type of power. Such a power is not only physical, it has a spiritual inspiration from inside which meets the life experiences on the outside to bring about the growth of human knowledge and a good human life.

I do not have any special reason to make modern people worship their ancestors. They are more than old copies to us, they are our old selves. But certainly the first human being who carried the spiritual symbol, Pang Gu, is worthy of respect as the model of our old Self. All people, regardless of race, who can develop spiritually must have had a spiritual source.

Nobody can argue whether modern people are descendants of the ancient people and whether the ancient people are descendants of nature. However, modern people with distorted knowledge might argue with the reality that nature is the first being.

There are three main theories that describe how the world has grown. They are the theory of evolution, theory of creation and theory of development. I do not need to explain Darwin's theory of evolution, because people already know it.

I believe that the people in the world are usually divided into two groups. One group of religious believers think that we were created by a big, powerful human-like God-being. The other group believes in the modern theory of evolution. After Darwin published his theory of evolution, people came to view life differently and many people exclusively follow that type of thought. The two groups have become enemies.

But there is another type of thought that is different from those two opposing types of thoughts. It is the theory of development. The development theory describes internal development. Once internal development comes to a new stage of maturity, then external development is needed. The original shape cannot carry the internal energy any more, so it needs to be reshaped. Therefore, a new species of life comes. Through years, through different stages of internal development, a human life also shapes itself differently. Human life did not develop from monkeys, nor was it created by somebody. Originally, it was a simple spiritual energy which integrated with material energy. During the next step, the internal energy grew, then the external shape could not function or carry it any more, so further change and development arose. But instead of changing externally or physically, we humans changed functionally. Regarding the basic shape, we have not changed much, but our functions have developed differently.

For example, 10,000 years ago, our original ancestors had two hands with ten fingers. Today, human people still have ten fingers. Ten thousand years ago, because of the level of their internal development, women could only put together an animal hide or fur to hang on the body for warmth and protection in winter. In summer, clothing made of leaves was worn. Only simple clothing that was draped or hung on the body could be made.

Now let us talk about 1,000 years ago in China. The women at that time did beautiful embroidery on silk clothing. It became an art.

Thus, the ten fingers of 10,000 years ago, and those same ten fingers 1,000 years ago, each had the same shape. Maybe they looked rougher before, but mostly the change was internal and invisible. Internal change makes the external expression different. The skill is different. This is the Taoist theory of development.

When life began on earth, the spirits, as natural essence, shaped themselves in each type of natural environment. It took a long time for the spirits to go through the difficult process of shaping themselves with physical forms. A great variety of forms were tried in accordance with the variety of natural habitats and climates on earth. It was when the human shape was developed that the spirits learned something practical: it is not necessary or appropriate to always change to a new shape to adapt to each different type of environment. With the human form, the spirits learned how internal spiritual development alone could bring harmony with a new external environment without the need to form a new physical shape.

The seeds that were originally sent down from Heaven express natural essence. The seeds are nurtured by natural vitality. There are no souls in the seaweed stage but there are in dinosaurs. The shape of all creatures follows the law of evolution and continues changing as an internal reaction to external life circumstances. As internal energy responded to life experiences, the soul of life started to evolve. Thus, the soul of a dinosaur and the soul of a monkey are different. The human soul is a further latecomer. Long ago, animal souls evolved into human bodies, but their animal response remained strong. Thus, it takes them a long time to overcome their animal tendencies to evolve to higher development. Thus, it takes longer for a human soul to reach its perfection or completion than other beings on the earth. Physical and spiritual evolution are comparable, but spiritual evolution is much more advanced.

When life developed on earth, human beings were one of the many types of creatures developed by the spirits. However, because we have the potential for internal spiritual growth, and because we are still related to the original, natural spiritual source, we are different from the other creatures. We can still reach that source. There is no prepared or predesigned plan for the development of nature; nature itself develops step by step. I mean, nature is the manifestation of its own essence. People are a manifestation of nature; thus, they also develop in a way that is not prepared or predesigned. For example, around 2,000 years ago, there was a young man who was chief of a village. He was a rascal type of person, and liked wine. He liked to have lots of fun; he was that type of person. But he was also adventurous. Later, he fought and defeated the first emperor of the strong United Kingdom under Ching Szu Huan and he become the founder of the second big dynasty in China. Such an event is not predesigned or predetermined. There is only potential for it to happen. Even if the potential is there, one never knows until it happens. This was what happened. Nobody planned that he would achieve that distinction from all the others, not his parents or anyone else.

Now I would like to give an example that illustrates that internal potential is not limited by outer shape. In the old type of Chinese society, a young man was born into a poor family. He had several brothers, and all of them were looking how to earn a good living. Because they were poor, the father and mother could not sustain so many children, so one boy was sent to an opera school, one was sent to be an assistant to a businessman, and one became a laborer in the harbor. Several decades later, one son had become a nationally famous opera performer and made lots of money, enjoyed a good life and was admired by many fans. The second brother, who was an assistant to a businessman, worked so diligently and earnestly that the businessman married him to his only daughter and let him continue his business. He turned out to be a multimillionaire. As for the laborer who worked in the harbor, he later became a manager who had hundreds of thousands of laborers working under him.

If someone were to exchange the positions of the three sons so that the businessman's son-in-law did labor work and the opera son became a businessman, etc., the development of each would be different. This would happen because the potential of each was different. However, good potential can develop more fully and easily than insufficient potential. Someone who has good potential might do well in many different fields. In some families, the sons all look exactly alike. If they stand next to each other and wear similar clothing, you cannot tell them apart. If you could observe the potential or internal form of each of them, you might see something different for each one.

Development makes one person different from another. Truthfully, people cannot be judged by their appearance, but the intellectual education of today just looks at the shape without working to develop the spiritual potential of its students. I admire modern people who can make canned pineapple; all the cans are the same, so people enjoy the same thing. However, they apply this same principle of uniformity to doctors, students and soldiers. They make them uniform like canned pineapple. They overlook that they are human beings with different spiritual potential.

For example, you can make training or education uniform for young people, but some will become soldiers or generals and some will become traitors. It is the internal potential that develops people differently.

Nowadays people like to control everything, but what can be controlled? People feel frustrated sometimes about their failures. Sometimes it is because they are trying to control a situation too tightly and not giving it enough room to develop naturally. Often they are trying to succeed in areas that are not in accordance with their internal potential. Balanced growth requires the inter-relationship and inter-dependence of the two sides of the brain or earth that can bring about good control and great success. The two sides of the brain are similar to the two hemispheres of the globe. The short-coming of the eastern side of the globe and the right side of the brain is that the interior is overly stressed. For example, Oriental people, especially Chinese people, mostly value what is inside. The western side of the globe or the left side of the brain overemphasizes and overvalues the outside shape. For example, Western people, especially American people, mostly value material possessions. The transition from "potential" into "balanced growth" is spiritual self cultivation.

If a person is too external, he neglects to achieve internal-ly. If a person is too internal, then he neglects to achieve externally. Both kinds of achievement are necessary for balanced growth. Mostly our western society values what is external. The external world and its development is impor-tant. However, the internal is also important. A person can put something in a beautiful box, but the beauty of the box will not increase the true value of its contents. Equally, a valuable item is not diminished in value by being wrapped in ordinary paper.

Sometimes, the internal is more important and at other times the external is more important. Usually an older person, after living life correctly, is more interested in the internal or spiritual. But for most people, the balanced way is best. If a person has a great spirit, yet lacks external development, skills, or resources to manifest that good energy in a positive, creative project, it is wasted.

The work on your soul is more important than merely working on a beautiful body. We all like to have beautiful bodies. But it might be dangerous to go along with a person who has a beautiful body but not a beautiful soul. I like both together.

In summary, we see that humans grow by creation and evolution. In the development of nature, there is no predesigned blueprint. Religious believers always think that a blueprint design was made before a human was born. Although to some extent a person's fortune can be told, the destiny of the individual is determined at the time the soul is shaped. One's destiny is the natural inclination of the individual. It is only a rough sketch of the person's personality and events in his life, and it can be altered by filling life with good details by individual subjective effort of spiritual refinement.

Q: Do you mean that the person's destiny is shaped when his soul is shaped? Would that be at birth?

Master Ni: No matter when it is shaped, destiny is not lasting. What is programmed can be deprogrammed. The soul picks up its destiny at the time the human body is born. When the soul leaves the body, destiny has no further relevance to the soul. It enters a different network.

Most people study both the theory of creation and the theory of evolution; but they are only observing the external things. Our tradition observed the internal change and developed its theory from there. No one knows when the universe started or when nature started, but one cannot deny that natural vitality is the main power of the entire universe. Natural vitality combines with the different material elements of a situation to produce changes.

The natural vitality or energy has intercourse with different natural environments. The combination produces various expressions or manifestations. For example, in a pond you find a water lily. Can anyone find a water lily in the ocean? No, but in the ocean one can find jellyfish spread out like big leaves. Can anyone find jellyfish in a pond? No, it is not possible.

Birds are the life expression of trees and the forest. In northern China, vultures used to prosper. Now, it seems they are almost extinct, so people are going to save them. However, if their natural environment, the forest, is not saved, all the birds will either go away or become extinct. We see that in different natural environments, we find different expressions of life and nature.

Human life is an expression of natural vitality. It is the highest natural expression. Human life is natural life, so people who think that God or nature is something far away from human people are totally mistaken. The connection of the concept of God with the concept of natural vitality has been discussed in my lectures.[1] Human life is at least the spiritual sign of nature. It is the essence of the material substance of nature. Human life is the highest expression of life.

Life manifests in many types of movement in the universe. All different forms of life are a model of nature. The sun, moon and stars each have their own types of form and movement. Trees move too, but much differently than the heavenly bodies. Animals are also varied in their abilities. The human being, however, is the best model of nature, because it can move so freely with its three spheres of body, mind and spirit. When a soul has an opportunity to enter a human life, it has received a special privilege.

A human life is so much more than just living from hand to mouth. A person can bring so much more than just food into his life if he wishes. A human has hands that bring food to feed his belly. His head, by thinking how to obtain the food, serves the body. The body, by processing the food, serves the head. They are totally connected. From the supposed order that the head serves the body, you see God serves life. From the supposed order that the body serves the head, you see that life serves God. The great connection is

---

[1] Please read my works, *The Power of Natural Healing* and *Harmony: The Art of Life.*

made by the nature of life whether from the order of head and hands or god and life. When the head serves the body, it is God serving life. When the body serves the head, it is life serving God. The great connection is made when the spirit of the life and the physical foundation of life has attained beautiful harmony.

How do human people serve God? By doing decent work and only doing as much as they can do well, by being receptive to what comes to them, and by accepting their life as it is. By this I mean, by not doing immoral work, not overextending themselves, not being aggressive and not taking opportunities away from the people for whom they are meant. Whatever can be brought about by the hand and mind to sustain life with decency is the best way to serve the individual divinity within.

Each individual divinity is connected with the divinity of the universe. Individual divinity is the center as the same as the function of that in nature. However, individual minds differ from one another, and often develop differently. When an individual is separated from his own divinity, internally he feels as though there is a constant fight. It is a fight between the mind and body. The spirit is locked in the body, and it does not fight. It is interesting to see that human life can project an image outside of itself and call that shadow or image as the divine God, yet people neglect their own divinity. The one who cannot relate to the divinity within him does not yet truly know God. If a person is outwardly religious but does not reach his own spiritual essence of life, one would consider him to be unspiritual, irreligious and unnatural. On the other hand, those people who develop themselves and nurture themselves as the internal essence of the external environment are true children of nature.

The meeting together of the three partners, body, mind and spirit, within a human life is not forever, unless a person practices a special cultivation. This cultivation makes his internal arrangement correctly ordered: spiritual light on the top, mind in the middle and the physical foundation or heavy part on the bottom. That is the right order of life. Do not put the soul at the bottom and the heavy level or physical sphere of life on the top: that would be the opposite order, making an inverted pyramid. That is opposite of the natural order of life. The essence of life maintains the life. By this I mean, the spiritual function maintains the life. It is not the quantity of years one has or having many material possessions that makes a life full and complete. Surely any person can produce or possess more. It is most beneficial to create and use the right quantity. Each person can only enjoy the amount that is right for him. Owning more or less than that is not beneficial. Not only is that true of possessions, it is also true of energy. Spiritually, one must learn to regulate the amount of one's energy, and also where it goes. For example, if a person can avoid putting too much energy out into worldly pursuits, he can nurture the internal, high spiritual essence. A certain quality of life comes from learning how to settle down within oneself. This is experiencing one's own energy instead of continually looking for energy from external, secondary sources which are so often unreliable anyway.

There is a practice that we once mentioned that can help a person's soul. In the book, *Internal Spiritual Growth Through Tao*, there is a chapter in which a group of people discuss different religious customs. There we talk about the Taoist secret of the mystical pass. That is a sensitive spot for each individual, because it is one of the higher spiritual centers. That is a helpful practice that each one can do for himself. Nowadays, it is hard to find a responsible, moral teacher to give you great spiritual benefit which is produced by his own cultivation. So you can do the practice yourself. It is better for you to not relate too closely with a teacher or a person who might really bring spiritual harm to you. If someone does this practice for you, they link their spiritual energy with yours when touching the mystical pass. So do it yourself.

Firstly, a person who wishes to do this practice must accept the Heavenly Way as his spiritual guidance. It brings him to Heaven. I do not mean that a person has to exactly fulfill everything mentioned in my book, *The Key to Good Fortune: Refining Your Spirit* or *The Heavenly Way*. It means that a person must accept the general principles laid down in the book as his way of life. Mostly that means to live a life that is helpful to other people.

The following practice is available to all people looking for spiritual growth, with no age or gender conditions. There is no special charge or personal obligation involved in doing this practice. I would like you to do it on a day of strong natural energy, like one of the equinoxes or solstices.

Before or just at sunrise, face the rising sun in the east. Put your two hands together, and using your right palm to hold the left hand which is in a fist (or left palm to hold right

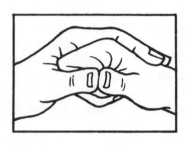

hand), making the two thumbs connect thumbprint to thumbprint, as in the illustration. Use the tip of the middle finger of the left or right hand to gently touch that center, the mystical pass, which is located in the area between the two eyebrows and two eyes. You only need to do it once, and it does not matter if you stand or sit to do this. You do not need to say or think anything special. It only takes about 5 seconds.

You can let other people do that service for you, a teacher or someone you trust. Sometimes a group of people do that practice in a spiritual gathering for this specific purpose. An associated custom to this practice includes the spiritual refreshment of eating bean soup. The purpose of this practice is to provide the spiritual opportunity to return new life.

Group practice, is usually done with a family, husband, wife and children or some spiritual friends. An offering can be made of fresh flowers and fragrant tea. Incense can be burnt. Some lines from the *Tao Teh Ching* may be read aloud:

"*The heavenly way is the spiritual awareness of*
*   the ancient developed ones.*
It is the spiritual enlightenment that
*   the precious individuals have passed down to all of us.*
It is not external establishment.
It is the guidepost of self-spiritual cultivation."

From Lao Tzu's *Tao Teh Ching*, other invaluable lines were given:

"The heavenly way is quiet,
yet it responds unfailingly.
The heavenly way does not require
that you ask it for help,
yet it reaches you without obstruction.
The heavenly way is widely embracing,
yet no one is neglected.
The heavenly way is vastly open,
yet no one can escape its justice.

The heavenly way is exemplified by stretching a bow.
The high side is lowered, the lower one raised;
The long section is shortened
and the narrow one widened.
The heavenly way always benefits others
and gives no harm.
The heavenly way helps the excessive
serve the insufficient.
The way of people is otherwise."

The later sages explained:

Intelligence, wealth, social power, good skills and physical strength can all be forms of excess.

It is the Heavenly Way that through one's spiritual awareness, help is given to the needy.

The way of people is opposite, making the less intelligent, less wealthy, less powerful, less skillful and less strong serve the one who already has more.

The wise Chuang Tzu addressed the former as "the student of nature" and the latter as "the student of distorted people."

The virtuous fulfillment of a student of Heaven is to follow his own spiritual awareness to give help to others.

Sages who follow the Heavenly Way give, but do not contend.

The one who has learned more shall give help to the one who has learned less.

The one who has achieved more can help the ones who have achieved less.

When the Heavenly Way is applied, it is with no private interest or selfish end.

The Heavenly Way is always with people who are upright and righteous.

Then, when this is fulfilled, we all live in the Heavenly Way.

When the friend, who out of spiritual self-awareness chooses to be the student of Heaven, opens the mystical pass, the high pass of the soul, the soul of this person is Heavenly saved. Be the seed of Heaven, and the seed of eternal life."

Then apply the touch to the person.

With this opportunity, a person can seriously follow the Heavenly way.[2] In the Taoist tradition, the learning of Tao is not a rigid process, but must be adjusted, reasonably, by and for the individual. By conforming one's life to the principles of the Heavenly Way, the person will be sure to grow with the third or the second kind of spiritual fruit as described in the other chapters of this book. Searching for the first kind of spiritual fruit is also possible, but the requirements are higher, and one needs to learn from a teacher.

Usually after all is done, bean soup is served to the group. At the winter solstice, red bean soup with brown sugar is usually served. At the spring equinox, soybean or yellow bean soup is served. At the summer solstice, mung bean or green bean soup is served. At the autumn equinox, black bean soup is served. Eating bean soup after doing the practice is not necessary, it is only a social element of doing it in a group.

It is ancient knowledge that when a person is going to pass away, the soul of the person will leave the body. There are few apertures in the human body that can serve as the gate of the spirit through which the soul may exit. Usually

---

[2]Please also see my book: *The Heavenly Way* or the complete edition, which is entitled *The Key to Good Fortune: Refining Your Spirit.* These books will help you further understand the way of life.

the soul will leave the body through the eye or nostril, but through the nostril is most common. It is told that if a soul leaves the body through the eye or nostril, it will be reborn to human life. If the soul leaves the body from the openings in the lower part of the body, it suggests a hellish result or that the person will be reborn into a dumb animal life. Only a few spiritual persons who are born with the bones in their head already softened and ready to open; those who cultivate diligently in life can leave through the crown of the head or mystical pass. When the soul leaves their body, it just rushes out through the top of their head. Those people will become Heavenly beings. If they come back to the world again, they are balanced people.

In our tradition, we think that one point at the crown of the head and one point in the front of the head are considered as the mystical pass or the soul pass at the time when the soul leaves the body. Both the crown and the mystical pass are the soul pass for achieved souls. The crown is where one ascends to Heaven. The mystical pass is probably for coming back to be a king or sage. I believe that no person has the power to change the destiny of another person's soul. Because spiritual growth is each individual's own effort, however, a person can improve his own destiny by taking the suggestion to perform the opening of the mystical pass. It is often better for someone with a balanced personality and spiritual cultivation to help you open your spiritual channels. However, a kind hearted, respectful person with the knowledge of this practice can help you. I myself, my two sons and the mentors or teachers in different centers can do this for you as a service at no charge or obligation on some special occasions. Generally, it is done during a special gathering.

Q: So through meditation a person achieves being able to pass through the crown and ascends to Heaven?

Master Ni: Not always. Ascending to Heaven by exiting the body through the crown practically means being an immortal with absolute freedom. Going through the mystical pass in the front of the head is a different level. On this level, the soul would still be attached to formed life and great worldly accomplishment.

It is an ancient spiritual secret that both can be achieved naturally and spiritually without the need of relying on religious teachings. Spiritual self-discipline, virtuous fulfillment and secret good deeds mean more than any externally established teachings. Especially the higher achievement must be higher than what the religions teach. The ancient Taoists courageously achieved themselves through independent life and self-spiritual cultivation.

The souls of most people leave through the eye. When they die, the scatteredness of spiritual energy can be observed in the enlarged pupil of the eyes. Nostrils, ears or mouth can all be used for the soul pass during the soul's withdrawal from physical life. They would still return to worldly life. Only the soul that ascends to the crown can fly out and reach as far as it can into the heavens.

A soul can also leave the body from the vagina, penis or anus. Passing through those apertures means sinking and the soul will suffer and come back to live a life as an animal, like a rat, pig or dog. I do not mean pampered American dogs, I mean Cantonese or Korean dogs who truly live a lowly dog's life and can be killed and eaten. It is spiritual truth that nobody can afford to be without developing its soul, or at least maintain the soul pure with all good potential. This is the essence of traditional spiritual teaching beyond different conceptual formalizations.

For high achievement, there are two things involved in one's practical cultivation. One to open the high channels. With the channels open, you have the possibility to go through to the high spiritual realm. Second, you must cultivate your spiritual energy to be strong enough to use the pass. You can be helped somewhat by a developed teacher to open the higher channels, but the second part you must do totally by yourself. Where people go and what results for their personal soul is not known until death. You can observe the people in your surroundings. People push themselves to a destination which is not what they would choose if they were to attain spiritual knowledge.

There are always individuals belonging to different channels of spirit. However, it is important not to judge other people. It is forbidden because having such spiritual pride inevitably means that you are going to fall. The most important thing is to watch yourself, your heart, mind, behavior, speech, work, close relationships, income and what goes out. Those things are most individual, and no one can really help, so you need to take care of them yourself. On the general level, even among relatives, no help can be given. Only a serious spiritual group can help each other to a certain degree and on a certain level. You still need to mind your own spiritual cultivation; that is what helps you in the end and to start newly. Nobody, anywhere, decides where you shall go. The condition of your own spiritual energy and spiritual quality decides where you shall go.

Q: Master Ni, what happens spiritually at the moment of death?

Master Ni: For most people, close to the moment of death, when you stop breathing and when the disintegration is beginning, no matter who you are or how high your intellectual achievement, whether you are a believer or a non-believer of a spiritual world, you shall see in the dark shadows of your surroundings the beings who come to take you to where you belong. These beings would include the passed away good friends, enemies and people with whom you have had a positive or negative emotional attachment. Now they show you whether you have spiritual support or more troublemakers. At this time the troublemakers take you where you belong. They are not real ghosts; they are your own spiritual elements. You have never known that in the entire living world, the worst enemy you have had is yourself.

If you are achieved, during your lifetime in your spiritual cultivation, you have composed yourself and harmonized the spiritual energy you have gathered. If you are achieved, your soul is pure and light, so you are free to just fly away. You should clearly see if you have attained unity or still suffer conflict before that day comes to you. In your cultivation, you have done all the processes and all the things rather than waiting until the time you are ready to die and when there is no more chance to repair yourself from any sort of trouble. Your cultivation is how you test yourself and improve yourself spiritually.

When an achieved soul decides to leave the body, it must be early morning, anytime before noon or right at noon, because the achieved soul would ride the light of the sun or solar energy to start his journey. Sometimes there is spontaneous phenomenon such as some subtle light or colorful rays which can be seen, beautiful auras are spread and visible in the sky, sweet smells are noticed like burning incense or musical notes are heard in the surroundings. Other people who have cultivated themselves spiritually can experience such things by being physically around him.

Sometimes the achieved one's body disappears by vaporizing, or disappears in the coffin after being there for a period of three years. Sometimes the person directly flies up in the sky to accomplish the vaporizing process. The achieved one's body which is left behind sometimes shrinks to be smaller and is sometimes kept in a display cabinet. That happens mostly for religious promotion, and I call that the "left over value of a sage's shell." Maybe it is done by religions in the eastern countries to give the future comers some encouragement, but it hardly has anything to do with the ascending soul.

Q: So how is it that we can achieve highly? I do not know how to do it.

Master Ni: It is done through the law of spiritual correspondence. Let me explain.

In the universe, if there is not an objective authority which decides to reward or punish a person or the soul of a human person, then what determines who does well and who does poorly in life? What determines whether a person will be spiritually achieved to exit from the crown of the head or somewhere else? Truthfully, it is the subtle law of the universe. This subtle law exists everywhere and is the strongest law, although it is gentle and subtle compared to the laws of a community or society which usually have a specific purpose and are temporary.

This subtle law can sometimes be interpreted as the law of correspondence, or the law of spiritual correspondence when applied to people. Spiritual correspondence means spiritually "like attracts like," or "you are what your own spiritual formation is."

Spiritual correspondence means that whatever actions you perform, the thoughts you think, what unfinished business you hold in your subconscious mind, and how you project your conceptions through your speech and relationships - all those things combine to be what you really are. Because it is all subtle, no change can be made in your own thoughts, mind and speech unless you make it yourself. That means that no external source such as a teacher can help a lot; teachers can only give suggestions. The change must basically be from your own will or longing to do it for the improvement of your own life.

Thus in order to move from the dark to the light, downward to upward, or from any extreme to the upright centered way, no sage or divine one can help you, even though they wish they could. Why can't they help you? In front of the subtle law, every life being and spiritual being is equal, and each must do its own part. Each of us forms ourselves spiritually and practically.

Once you understand the law of spiritual correspondence, you know there is nobody who is responsible for the fruit of your life other than yourself. You grow your own life tree. You protect and nurture your own life tree. You can enjoy the fruit and share it with whomever you like.

So what you are is decided by the truth of your spiritual reality. I am not talking about being a man or woman, lawyer or Indian chief, old or young. I am talking about being truly happy inside or feeling miserable and depressed, being accepting of what life offers or cantankerous and resistant, being a loving person or always being afraid to enter into an intimate relationship. Each person is spiritually self responsible for one's own spiritual future and spiritual growth.

In everyday life, we can change our appearance by changing clothes, wearing wigs, coloring our hair, using cosmetics or special skills like plastic surgery; men can grow beards and moustaches or shave them off. But the spiritual reality of each individual is much deeper than what can be seen on the surface or exterior. A person cannot disguise or pretend that one's spiritual reality is different from what it actually is. However, during each lifetime, there is an opportunity to alter and improve our spiritual quality and reality through spiritual self-discipline and self-cultivation.

When close to death, if your brain is already hardened, and your heart and mind has lost the creative power, there is no time left for you to alter yourself. Summoning a priest to your deathbed to repent all your troubles and mistakes does not do a lot for a person, although for some it is a consolation. The only real possibility to make significant improvement in ourselves is to build ourselves in a spiritual direction during our lifetime and watch the life tree grow. We do this by learning to avoid things that are harmful for our own souls. We do it by starting right now.

External religions offer social discipline. They developed when people were somewhat wild in nature in their lives so something was organized for them. A really achieved one may or may not learn something about religious customs. Mainly an achieved one has learned to discipline oneself spiritually by seeing what is right.

The spiritual reality of a person is what really counts, not what religion he or she belongs to. Religion is not insurance that will give a payoff if you have an accident or make a mistake. Spiritual awakening gives a reward of a different kind. People awaken spiritually and work to develop their own soul and courageously develop themselves. The achievement of such a person is no less than that of any spiritual image projected by any religion. This is truthful and essential spiritual knowledge.

If you have been observing the people in your surroundings, you might make fast conclusions such as, "So and so is a bad person but enjoys his life the most." There would be troubles in so judging other people. One is you do not go deeply enough to see that a person's success must have been brought about by a number of good virtues so the person could bring about good fortune for himself.

Good virtues such as diligence, hard work, sincerity and continuing to learn, etc,, can bring success to a person. Even a person who is recognized as being a good or kind-hearted person, if he or she does not pay attention to what is happening every moment and every day, can fall into the trap of bad habits, shortcoming of bad disposition or choosing bad company. If a person does not adjust oneself to the working or living environment internally or externally, there will be hardly any way to avoid failure and troubles.

Originally, there is no such thing as a good person or bad person. Truthfully, there are only good virtues and spiritual pitfalls. A person must continually work to develop the good virtues and avoid the pitfalls to be able to appear as a good person. Otherwise, without constant self observation and evaluation, a person will appear to be corrupted like dirty water. Also, a good person can suffer. If failure happens there must have been an accumulation of small negligences in some area or perhaps it was time for change in a person's natural cycles.

So the decisive factor of one's spiritual future is to be watchful of yourself and the environment in which you find yourself. Basically, there is no boogey man to watch or discipline you. You must take spiritual responsibility to form and build yourself. If you can hold in your mind the truthful knowledge of the law of spiritual correspondence, you can understand how everybody brings about different fruit to his or her life. If a person cultivates one's positive attitudes with balanced thought, not only thinking of one's own benefit, and thereby becomes an upright person, he or she will bring the light energy to the head and the spiritual fruit of exiting through the crown to ascend to heaven is natural and likely.

In the spiritual world, it is you yourself who chooses the how and what in your life. Do not let anyone or anything pull down your spiritual self, but use them as a mirror to cultivate yourself. In other words, if you do not like the people you see in your life or if you do not like their behavior, that may be a definite clue that it is you who needs to do some work on yourself or make a change. Or if people are telling you something about yourself, perhaps you need to listen.

Judgement is not something that occurs after you die. Rather, spiritual correspondence is something that you live with every moment. It is universal spiritual reality as the law of spiritual correspondence. Our spiritual reality is what we are. Deeply, nobody can cheat anybody else, but on the spiritual level, people can only cheat themselves.

The only good choice is to nurture your great spirit, noble spirit and rich spirit. This can be done without having to struggle on the surface or being in competition for false flowers and fruit.

Chapter 7

Let Us All Return
To the Universal Soul

I have given the practice so that all of my friends and readers can reach their soul energy. You can reach it by doing the practice with sincerity and prudence. You will prove that it is not your imagination, but it is the subtle sphere of your life. Also, through detailed discussion, I have sketched the essence of the teachings about reaching the soul from all spiritual traditions. So finally, you have learned the correct way, as I have shown it to you. By comparing the various teachings, you can see from the different attempts, set-ups and viewpoints that you have received the correct understanding about the matter of reaching the soul. Now you can be sure, after following my instruction and doing what I have recommended, that you will bear your spiritual fruit, if you wish.

But in this moment, I need you to answer one question for me. You understand that your soul is part of life. It is the most essential, most important part of your life, although it is invisible in most normal circumstances. So if we have a soul, where can we meet our soul?

We have already said that it is not a matter of "if." If, by doing the practice, you have already discovered that you have a soul, then you also need to know the source, destination, support or sponsorship of the soul. That is important. This is something I have omitted until the last moment, so now we need to discuss it.

The entire universe, that which we call nature, is viewed by modern scientists as a mechanical operation or a big machine. But the reality known to all is that machines cannot give birth to life, unless you define your life as a machine. In today's world, machines can even create or bring about some product, but they cannot create a soul. Therefore, the mechanical view of the universe has something missing. It is not complete understanding. To understand completely, we still need to return to the understanding of the sages who accumulated more than two million years of living on earth. With their spiritual development, they understood one thing: the entire universe is one life. It is a life. It is organic. It is not mechanical. It has its soul. That soul is our common soul. So you have your individual soul, your friend has his soul, family members have their soul and all people in different countries have their souls. There is also a big soul, common to all. The common soul of nature is Tao. Tao is the common soul of all life. Tao is universal soul, the source of universal spiritual reality.

The ordinary external religions imagine that the universe has a ruler. The job of the ruler is to create everything by his own design. He needs to rule everything himself. Like a policeman, he watches your behavior and your life, and in any moment, he is ready to give you a ticket or some trouble. Practically, you have found out, by yourselves, that this mental creation came from the stage when human ancestors had not reached their maturity. Their imagination is interesting, but it is not close to the truth. Generally, when we think of a ruler, we think of someone who is a leader; someone in front, who is a governor, ruler or a guide. Let us take a constructive look at Tao. It leads the universe and the world, yet is unknowable by the conceptual mind. Chapter 14 of the *Tao Teh Ching* states:

> *There is something unseeable.*
> *It is called Yi.*
> *There is something inaudible.*
> *It is called Shi.*
> *There is something untouchable.*
> *It is called Vi.*
> *With these three different natures*
>   *that combine together as one,*
> *This something does not show brightly up above.*
> *It does not show darkness underneath.*
> *There is something uncontrollable and unnameable.*
> *Once we feel it is there,*
>   *it immediately returns to non-beingness.*
> *This something is the shape of the shapeless.*
> *It is the sign of the signless.*
> *It is evasive.*

It is elusive.
You cannot see its head.
You cannot see its rear.
What is it? What else in the world has that nature?
That is the soul of the universe
to be illustrated by the mind.

Chapter 25 of the *Tao Teh Ching* says,

There is something that converged long ago,
even before the birth of heaven and earth.
Lonely, quiet, independent and unaltered,
it circles around.
It is the mother of heaven and earth.
We do not know how to name it,
so we reluctantly call it Tao.

In this chapter, we see that Tao is the universal soul, the source of the universe. In the other chapters, we see that Tao gives birth to everything. What else gives birth to everything? We know we each have an individual soul. We also know that the great life of the universe has its own soul, its inexhaustible soul. That is our support. That is the final truthful source of our spiritual being. If anybody does not reach this subtle truth, origin and source, he may be externally strong, but his life is shallow. He does not reach the deep soul of life. Once I had reached some enlightenment, when I read this, I could not help but weep. I identified that it was me before I became a shaped life. Through all life experience, I certainly will return to it. It is my soul. It is yours, too. We all come from and return to it.

Tao, the universal soul, is described in the 21st chapter of the *Tao Teh Ching:*

Tao is something very evasive and very illusive.
However, among the evasiveness and illusiveness,
there is a certain sign.
From further evasiveness and elusiveness,
there is something.

It is uncontrollable,
*   but it is the subtle essence.*
This essence is truthful and very reliable.
Everything has changes.
Everything has a time to come and go,
*   but something of this something forever is there.*

Dear friends, I wish that you can learn how to reach your soul. You can also learn how to save and protect your soul. If you are wise enough and decisive enough, you will find the universal vitality that is also the universal soul. It is Tao. I recommend, with this understanding of the esoteric meaning, that you read over the *Tao Teh Ching*. It would be worth your time. I have translated and published it as a book, *The Complete Works of Lao Tzu*. There, I translated the word "Tao" as the "Integral Truth." However, if you change those words to be "universal soul," you will find that we are living in love, with the support and under the protection of Tao. Tao truly gives boundless grace to all. It is the mother of heaven, earth and people. It is the source of everything. It is definitely not limitable. In a different time, we called it the absolute, the ultimate or the infinite; do those words really describe anything?

Externally, you find the root of life from your physical father and mother. And who gave birth to them? Who gave birth to your great-great-great grandparents? They were evolved from another shape of life. That could be animals. Animal life evolved from vegetation. Vegetation evolved with the integration of water energy and sun energy. Where did the sun come from? Where did the water come from? Where did the earth come from? It is a big life, all the sizes of life came from the big life. The entire physical universe is its shell, the body of the universal soul.

Friends, you have lots of sincerity, devotion and love. You were misguided to believe the human conceptions that were made by the false establishment of external religion. You were mistaken in applying your emotion and love to a wrong object. Now come back; open your eyes to see the true mother who gives you life and love. Only when you find the universal soul does your life have a root. Otherwise, your life is just like duckweed floating over the water with no root. Traveling on the world, wandering on the surface of life, your life has no root. So dear friends, my work is to point out something missing in external religion, for the last two to three thousand years. You are wandering homeless. You do not know where your home is, what is your real name, your real source and who are your parents. You are lost.

. Please take some time to meditate on the *Tao Teh Ching*. The teaching of the *Tao Teh Ching* is so gentle, it is not forcefully presented, but it is the last truth. You need this truth to support your life and make you rationally strong. Because it is truth, it does not need strong words. It is truth with a gentle nature. It is the gentle virtue of the parents to bring the entire universe together without discrimination, without trying to see who is better, who is worse. It practices the principle of equality and impartial love. With the subtle teaching of Tao, you deeply root yourself in the source of the universe. Your soul is never lost again.

Dear friends, this is not my personal contribution. It is the truth that has been covered through thousands of years. Because we have been looking for an external force, this blocks the inner light. We cannot see and cannot reach our motherly love. From each word, sentence and chapter, you will find the teachings. The guidance is written for your eternal life.

Beloved friends, the human created "gods" are images of the human mind's own egotistic expression. All such gods are egomaniacs and work towards being competitive; they bring the world to war and chaos. There is no peace because they have not grown well. We might think of ourselves as one of the gods. We might think we are weaklings who need to rely on the external force to help us join the world of competition. That is not the truth we are looking for; that is not the truth that all humankind needs. That is the undeveloped ambition of establishing one race, one tribe or one single person above all the others. That is false teaching; it is not true teaching.

My beloved friends, you have your wisdom. You know the truth, you see the truth. Turn back from being astray. You are the stray puppy wandering around, who does not find your home. You have been wandering away from the right way. Now you are on the right path. This is the time to return. You have been lead astray by bad company and by imitating bad company. Come back to the real source of your truthful life.

Dear friends, why do you always discover that you are so unhappy? No matter how you reach out, it seems that whatever you do is to escape the loneliness, trouble and pain; that unnameable feeling of missing something in your mind. That is because you have not found your true spiritual source. Though in this moment I have pointed out your source, you still need cultivation to make the direct connection with the source. It is not the adoration of a person, a place or a nation. The truth is all people, all places and all nations. Then you shall be joyful, and have no more feeling of missing something. No need to do this or that, just to escape the unbearable emotional loneliness.

Remember, do not be misguided by emotional types of practice. The general religious emotional approach will cause separation from Tao. Only gentleness, quietude and sincerity will make you perfectly united with Tao.

Finally, you will find the source of your life. This is so important. Also, you do not know the right way to behave and how to live your life. You do not know what is right to pursue. When you reach the source, you will suddenly light up. You will see and know what is the right way to live your good life; how to behave. You will enjoy your life with the universal mother, the source of the universe.

Now, you have almost become complete. People feel incomplete because they have lost their connection with the universal root. Now you are almost complete again because finally you have reached the root of your life. You have received congratulations for taking a job, graduating from school, for your marriage, giving birth to children, but you have noticed that those things only make you happy for a while. Then they bring other obligations and tedious work again. But in this moment, you should really celebrate yourself for when and what you have and will reach, because you are meeting what you have been missing for so long. When you were born on the earth, it was as though you were being sent to a foreign country. There were no real friends or anyone close in that land. Now, finally, you see her again, the great mother of the universe.   How happy; what a great occasion for a special celebration.   The best celebration is to calm down and find a quiet place to read the *Tao Teh Ching*. Maybe you do not focus on the words, but what is behind the words.   They will carry you to see your mother.   Thank you.

Chapter 8

Let Your Natural Life Flow Like Water

A discussion with some visitors in Malibu.

Q: I know some people who are involved in cryonics. Cryonics is a study where doctors and scientists have developed a way to freeze the entire body to buy time to find cures for diseases such as cancer and AIDS. The doctors involved in such research know nothing about the soul. I would like to know what would happen to the soul in such a case.

Master Ni: Cryonics is a misbelief. Those doctors think that the physical body is the life. They do not know that the physical body is what the soul rides on; it is just a machine. Once the rider goes away, the machine no longer works. There is a difference between a young life suddenly buried under an avalanche and a dying life in which a soul has finished its journey. The soul of each individual is the boss. When people go to sleep, the main soul descends deeply within the body. Only when the soul comes to ride in our head do we awaken and function normally.

In ancient times, some serious spiritual students were not allowed to sleep. It was not external discipline - they did not allow themselves to really fall asleep, for two reasons. One reason was that maybe some external spirits would invade the body. Another reason was that if the soul leaves the upper center of the body, all the functions of the body slow down. It is equal to slow death.

Q: So another spirit could come in?

Master Ni: Yes. When I first came to the United States, a friend told me a rumor about Walt Disney. I do not know if it is true. My friend said that before Mr. Disney had cancer and died, he asked and accepted the treatment to be frozen in this way. So this person, if he can still be considered a person, is now in a refrigerator. People do not know that even if you keep the body, there is no use unless the soul is with it. That type of thing is totally different from serious spiritual practice. Spiritual practice preserves your soul. At any time when it is right for a change, a spiritual being can take a new, refreshed flesh being. So thoughts of keeping the body without taking care of the soul are from people who do not have complete knowledge about life.

Q: It could be dangerous.

Master Ni: Dangerous and useless. It is not meaningful in preserving a good life.

Q: How often should one use the I Ching *or consult it?*

Master Ni: There are two ways to use it. One way is to use it if you wish to use the reflecting function of your mind. It is a way to train your reflecting, because the answers you receive will not be intellectual. Intellectually, we think. By consulting the *I Ching*, perhaps you can find out if the answer is similar to your thoughts - the expected suggestion - and whether you are on the right track in your movement. So if you wish to train the reflecting function of the mind, which may also be what they call the subconscious, then you might frequently consult the *I Ching*.

The other way to use the *I Ching* is merely to read from it every day. You do not need to do any divination. By reading from it, your mind will unconsciously be trained to be flexible. Then whenever any kind of situation comes, you will find that you already know the answer. You will not need to look for the lines at that time because all the lines are already programmed in your brain. The answer is in there already.

There are different ways to do it.

Q: What can one do, aside from eating practices and Chi Kung (Chi Gong) and T'ai Chi Movement, to continue learning spiritual practices without a teacher nearby. In Seattle, we do not have anyone to teach us more spiritual or Taoist practices to incorporate on a daily level.

Master Ni: When I write books, I consider that I cannot be everywhere physically.   The books are what I offer to people who wish to help themselves.   But I will suggest that people who have a similar quest in mind organize a study group. For example, after the T'ai Chi Movement class in Los Angeles, they have a gathering.   Questions come from people and answers come from people.   Constantly using the books makes them an inspiration and a confirmation of your own answer, the one that came from within yourself. In that way, you do not need a teacher; you can use the books and also help each other.

In general, why do I write?   Because a teacher will usually give you a good answer, but he or she will also habitually manage your mind.   Sometimes a student may have trouble when looking for a good answer, and cannot find it within himself.   If the person who is acting as the teacher has a special intention, they may give you an answer based on circumstances.   If it is the wrong answer for your question, you will be troubled.

There was a group called "The Temple of the People" which had a leader who guided all its followers to move from California to New Guinea.   Why did so many people listen to him, and take the poison down there?   The reason is the trust, the faith that was built every day and night. So many people had total trust in that person.   People still thought the person was sane, good, sound and spiritual; they did not know that the individual had already changed. From one bad instruction, all the people suffered.   This type of thing has happened repeatedly in history with all kinds of religious leadership.   This is why your own singular spiritual growth is better and more trustworthy than any other spiritual individual who is called master or teacher.   Maybe sometimes they will mislead you, or you will simply fail to understand them.

Q: *You are the only teacher that I have had since my youth that I have trusted.*

Master Ni: Thank you. I also keep open to see what you can bring in to inspire me in my work.

Q: So in terms of doing discipline . . .

Master Ni: When I met you in California, I already knew you had lots of capability for social leadership. Yes, we live in the world, so we need a good goal and purpose in life to exercise our good energy. Otherwise our good energy is wasted. You are not trained to live in monasteries or caves or follow a teacher. But because you have a capability for leadership, you can still be a spiritual teacher, because you have adopted good spiritual material. You do not need to be a channel or a medium, but only be a good channel of the written words. It is much better to be earnest and teach from a book than be like those people who try to fake channeling and say they are channeling a certain spirit. That is not a good way to teach.

So I would like both of you, on the side, to consider that the best way to help the needs and problems of your friends is to start a study group, to discuss and share what you have learned from the books. Each week, meet in a certain place, a home or someplace, and do just that. Then you will feel you have really made true friends. Also, your world will develop everyday, and not only for the purpose of business.

Teaching is like using medication, food or food supplements. It is still under your own estimation. Sometimes you feel good, sometimes you feel bad; what is the reason? If you always make your spirit alert, your spiritual sensitivity and alertness will always be developing.

Q: When acting, on a stage or other performance, is it a good idea to use spiritual energy?

Master Ni: Acting is more emotional. If an actor or a singer is not emotional, he or she cannot stir up people's interest. Now, to make good use of acting, we might ask ourselves: can the story I am acting inspire people to become a good person or not?

Q: What I do before a scene is this: I see the energy connecting to the world, and that is not too much effort. But my mind usually gets in the way. When my mind gets in the way, no emotions come. So I connect like this, and I find it easier. Is that spiritual energy?

Master Ni: That is one way to manage personal energy when acting; maybe it is a good way. Acting can be considered a service, but that depends on the individual. John Wayne, for example, during his whole life, always acted the part of a good person. He made an image and always let the movie watchers know that the bad people will always be punished in the end. It is a good message to that level. You cannot say it is not a service. Just look at what message you are giving. Usually an actress gives a mixed message, so when you choose a role, choose a good story.

Q: There are rhythms of the earth, there are times of day that are best to take energy and when it is most available. Also there are times of the day when different organs are best reached. I mean the different systems, the five elements within the body. If you have written about it, I have missed those sections, about the different times of day.

Master Ni: I have recently written a book called, *The Story of Two Kingdoms*. Maybe it will be helpful in your search for some information about spiritual cultivation. Generally speaking, in the early morning the energy is stronger than at other times.

Q: What hours?

Master Ni: Some people are not serious spiritually, and because they have social or business obligations, they miss it. The best time is from 3:00 to 5:00, but usually most people cannot use it. For example, when I am on a trip, I cannot use it either. If you cannot get up that early, then whenever you get up is an appropriate time, as long as it is before sunrise. We welcome the sun rising. At that hour, the energy is strong, because it comes from the sun.

Q: We can arrange our schedule to do that.

Master Ni: Yes, I think now you can arrange that. Before also.

Q: It was not so easy before. At different times of the day, when different organs . . .

Master Ni: There is a formality called Tzu Wu Liu Chu, which is the circulation. The middle points are midnight and midday. Tzu Wu Liu Chu describes the circulation of energy through different organs. This knowledge of life circulation is information that has been set up for the purposes of acupuncture and spiritual cultivation. Let us say, for example, that you have lung trouble. During the early morning hours from 3:00 to 5:00, the energy is beneficial and usually helps your lung. At that time, you can take care of your lungs by drinking herb tea, doing special exercises or breathing practice. That is the best hour. Accordingly, different organs have a different beneficial and more effective hour to do such practices, which usually is better for it. It is too complicated for most people who have no knowledge of these things.

However, for anybody who wishes revitalization or regeneration, I think that early morning is still the best time.

Q: My girl friend seems to have liver problems. What hour is good for that and what should she do?

Master Ni: Is the liver problem from emotions, or what is the cause? You first need to figure that out.

Q: I had hepatitis in India in 1983, and since then, my digestion has not been very good.

Master Ni: Many people come back from India sick from the special parasites. It would be better for you to go to my son, Maoshing, to fix the trouble. This has to be fixed. It is a whole life problem. It cannot be cured. It can reoccur at any time, so it has to be treated 100% seriously. Do not take it lightly.

Q: It is true, I feel it gets better and then worse. But I feel that the physical affects the emotional. Sometimes my physical body starts feeling bad and then my emotions, even if my mind tries to calm down my emotion...

Master Ni: I understand. It is better not to have that problem. Once you have that problem, you have to be serious and do something about it.

Q: I think I want to learn more about some specific practices like breathing practices. All we ever learned was from one man who taught us some Chi Kung exercises. He called them moving meditation and eight treasures. But yesterday at the class I saw the way Maoshing and your students do the Eight Treasures and it is not at all the same. I want to have something so that when I wake up in the early morning I can work with energy and also with breathing. How and where does one learn that?

Master Ni: My system is passed down from the truly achieved Taoist immortals. It is quite different. However you do it, it is still a good thing. Mao made a videotape of the Eight Treasures. You can learn from that. Also there is a videotape for Chi Kung. Breathing is also an organized system.

Q: The first time I read one of your books, there was a section on different styles of T'ai Chi Movement and it was very relevant. I want to learn something to do. Just living one's life is not enough.

Master Ni: I hope to have time to make some videos, because although I am agreeable to many styles of T'ai Chi Movement, it is true that some can help people more than others.[1] A lifetime is not very long, and the energy is not very much. You can only have time to pick up the best things to learn and to have. It is not beneficial to keep all the books. Only a few books are beneficial to keep as friends. For example, if you go to a jewelry store, you see many different pieces of jewelry, but you would not like to own and use all of them. You would only select the best ones. What is best is not necessarily judged according to the price someone has put on it, right? Learning some practices is just like that.

Many people say that in Taoism there are truly lots of secrets. But mostly it is a matter of your appreciation, and if you know the right thing to pick up. That is important.

So if I have a chance, I will make some videotapes. I would like to have your sister accompany me in the videotape, because her beauty can attract more business!

Q: It was a special treat to watch you yesterday when you were doing T'ai Chi Movement. Your beauty is hard to compare to. It was really like water. I could see your inner bliss.

Master Ni: Thank you.

---

[1]Videotapes now or soon available include the Eight Treasures and Unity T'ai Chi Movement by Maoshing Ni, Crane Style Chi Kung by Daoshing Ni, and Dao-In, Gentle Path T'ai Chi Movement, Sky Journey T'ai Chi Movement, Infinite Expansion T'ai Chi Movement and Cosmic Tour T'ai Chi Movement by Master Ni.

Chapter 9

The Pursuit of Free Soul

1

Let me say to the truth seekers:
*   you are exhausting yourself.*
Each person has his own spiritual essence,
*   which cannot be described by words,*
*   yet is responsive to all.*
It hides itself in form,
*   but remains formless.*
Learn to take care of it.
Do not color it and confuse yourself.

2

Here is a big cave for my home.
There is nothing in the cave.
It is spacious and clean.
It is as bright as though under the sun and the moon.
With simple food, my body is sustained.
With simple clothes, the illusive life is covered.
Though there are abundant wonders from many sages,
*   I cherish being with original nature.*

3

There is one of precious nature,
*   who lives alone.*
He cannot be sought.
He enters and exits without the need of a door.
He can be the size of an inch,
*   or even smaller.*
He can be big enough to be everywhere.
If you do not accept this truth of life,
You forever miss it and cannot meet it again.

4

I have a pearl.
It has been buried a long time.
Nobody knows where.

Have you seen the moonlight?
It lights up the whole sky.
It hangs up there,
Beautiful and bright!
People see it wax and wane.
I see no change.
It resembles this pearl of mine,
staying on high, with no variation of day or night.

5

The holy mountain is very high.
There are no roads to get there.
Only the one who has attained Tao,
who can ride on the vehicle of nonbeing.
can be there and enjoy.

6

I have my precious sword;
it is very sharp.
It is not made of worldly metal.
Once it is accomplished, it needs no more sharpening.
It is as bright as the white snow.
It shines through all the clouds.
The sharp blade disperses any obstacle.
I carry it with me everywhere
but it cannot be seen by the fool.

7

I have my script.
It is very secret and sacred.
It has no shape and title.

No other can reach it.
No other can learn from it.
The one who can reach it
Must know the life of no form.

8

I live on the cold mountain.
Against the steep rock I stay and rest
Far away from all annoyance.
When I gather my pearl, it can be seen by none.
When I release my pearl, it reaches all.
Its light shines brilliantly upon my own mind.
No sacred words can be used to describe it.
It is my precious pearl.

9

It is pure
    to go nowhere and to come nowhere.
It does not stay
    inside, outside and the middle.
It is spotless like a crystal.
The full light
    goes beyond the sky.

10

When you see things,
    like see nothing.
When you hear things
    like hear nothing.
When you feel happy
    like feel nothing.
When you feel angry
    like feel nothing.
Everything returns to its source.
You transcend the formed being of all life.

11

You are perplexed by your own desire and love;
  it is hot and fast-burning like the fire.
When you are awake
  the fire turns to ash.
Fire and ash
  come from the same source.
When all false covering is removed
  the truth of simple essence is seen.

12

Set no conscious mind at anything.
Allow all in activity in your surroundings.
The wooden cow is not scared
  when the lion roars.
The robot is not moved
  by seeing beautiful flowers and birds.
The mind of an achieved person
  is not sentimental.
Flowers and birds are not scared by his presence.
Have a conscious mind like that.
What is the worry when the wisdom of transcendence
  is at its growth.

The free soul is the achievement of the learning of Tao.
The free soul can be achieved by conceptual freedom, psychological maturity, emotional detachment from all things
and embracing the spiritually unadorned, simple essence.
The flying soul is achieved by internal energy sublimation,
transformation and evolution. The flying soul is the spiritual enterprise of the ambitious Taoists. They follow the
experience and methods developed by the ancient achieved
ones who eventually flew to the stars, constellations and
northern star systems. Most life beings in outer space are
formed purely from chi particles by reason of their
unfleshly environment. Human beings resulted from the
intercourse of these Heavenly energies and the earthly energy. Human life was initiated on the earth as a flesh body
formed with the cooperation of the heavenly spirits (Hun)

and the earthly spirits (Po). Life is the integration of both, while death is the disintegration of both. Spiritual immortality is achieved through the further evolution of this new species, human life. When one has become ready or evolved through the achievement of his spiritual cultivation during his lifetime, death is not disintegration; it is the new life of exuviation. At his death, there is no disintegration. Instead, the higher, subtle essence accomplishes further integration and convergence with the earthly elements. The union of the two creates a new, immortal flying soul which can go anywhere it wishes.

Many material, social, political and spiritual achievements were accomplished through the help, inspiration, and experience of the immortals. Also, the contribution of the spirits or souls of our human ancestors cannot be neglected in our practical life.

The cultivation of the free soul is the foundation for the achieving of the flying immortal soul. Though it can be attained by people of natural mind, as spiritual learning and practice, the achievement of the flying immortal soul is more serious than the attainment of the free soul. I would think that it is a special goal or reward for a number of people. However, it is a spiritual law that only those who have done great, or many small, good deeds in ordinary society are qualified to obtain the opportunity to learn such a precious thing. Traditionally, one is supposed to have done 3,000 good deeds or have benefitted 3,000 lives by one's single life. Usually, human society does not focus on such learning. For those who are ready to learn, the goal of ordinary human society and the life of spiritual people can be guided by *The Book of Changes and the Unchanging Truth, The Complete Works of Lao Tzu, The Uncharted Voyage toward the Subtle Light, The Footsteps of the Mystical Child, The Gentle Path of Spiritual Progress, The Way of Integral Life, Stepping Stones for Spiritual Success, Eight Thousand Years of Wisdom, The Key to Good Fortune: Refining Your Spirit (The Heavenly Way), Tao, the Subtle Universal Law,* and my other books. My recent publications take the essence of the natural spiritual background through millions of years of human life from the dark to the light. Personal spiritual development is the most important enterprise in which a person can invest his time, energy and direction of life. Any person who can further learn the essence of those teachings and apply them in his life may receive the spiritual reward of not needing specific cultivation to achieve spiritual immortality. At the least, there are no more obstacles created by oneself in living such a way. Surely, you then belong to Heaven.

Student E: Master Ni, what is the meaning of the Chinese writing on the poster of Master Lu which we use together with the Workbook for Spiritual Development?

Master Ni: I wrote the following two poems in Chinese, as a student of universal spirituality, on the poster of Master Lu, Tung Ping. (The picture on the poster is also a likeness of me.)

I

"The Universe is one object.
The wholeness of time is one minute.
No way to split it apart.
All finds oneness in Tao."

II

"Do not mistake this one
        to be the great Master Lu, Tung Ping.
However, there is no difference between him
        and a modern student who achieves ascendence.
The beautiful scene in front of the pavilion of Yu Yang
        may also attract my enjoyment.
It was Master Lu who achieved
        and flew over Tung Ting Lake;
        it is no longer a single event
        after my achievement of the likeness.
The entire universe is as big
        as a grain of mustard seed as I view it.
The sun, the moon and the earth, all stretched out,
        are spread on a bit of my palm.

Consummate art may have done well
   in sketching Master Lu to exactness;
Still, how ever is it possible
   to paint the immortal essence on canvas?"

Conclusion

The purpose of my life is to continue the ageless evergreen wisdom of Tao. My life activities are the activities of universal natural truth. My life will be the continual unfoldment of the universal subtle law. My soul continues the evolution of the universal soul. My life is the unlimited exhibition of the integral truth. The condition of the world is the condition of my physics. I must work to reach its well-being, because the well-being of the world is the good support of my soul.

I will not keep looking for my personal salvation alone; such a thing does not exist as long as others are suffering. I will not keep searching for my personal individual delivery alone. Such a thing is unreal until the wisdom of all worldly people is improved and until all people live in the subtle light.

Physically, I have outgrown the shape of my childhood. Spiritually I have found the truth that inspires me for endless growth. I have purified all narrowness and prejudice from my conventional, non-fruitful and backward religious education. I cannot abandon the world to enjoy my spiritual life only. I am one of worldly life. The world is part of my life. I uphold my share of the responsibility to bring flower and fruit to all lives. Without the well-being of the world, one individual's prosperity is only a false paper flower. As long as I dedicate my life to the welfare of my own person and of all other human people, I will continue to grow. I dedicate my life to the limitless spiritual development of my self, not only to serve myself better but also to serve the world better. The world has helped me to develop, thus I am going to help the world develop. I dedicate my life to the common goal of total global progress without prejudice or discrimination. That is Tao.

I dedicate my never-tiring life to the learning of Tao. Then I can bring a good life, with the development of all three spheres, to myself and all my fellow people. Finally, I dedicate my life to bringing goodness, beauty and truth to myself and all other lives.

I would like to request that the readers of this book re-read the preface as an additional conclusion.

BOOKS IN ENGLISH BY MASTER NI

Quest of Soul - New Publication!
In Quest of Soul, Master Ni addresses many subjects relevant to understanding one's own soul, such as the religious concept of saving the soul, how to improve the quality of the personal soul, the high spiritual achievement of free soul, what happens spiritually at death and the universal soul. He guides the reader into deeper knowledge of oneself and inspires each individual to move forward to increase both one's own personal happiness and spiritual level. 152 pages. Stock No. BQUES Softcover, $11.95

Nurture Your Spirits - New Publication!
With truthful spiritual knowledge, you have better life attitudes that are more supportive to your existence. With truthful spiritual knowledge, nobody can cause you spiritual confusion. Where can you find such advantage? It would take a lifetime of development in a correct school, but such a school is not available. However, in this book, Master Ni breaks some spiritual prohibitions and presents the spiritual truth he has studied and proven. This truth may help you develop and nurture your own spirits, which are the truthful internal foundation of your life being. Taoism is educational; its purpose is not to group people and build social strength but to help each individual build one's own spiritual strength. 176 pages. Stock No. BNURT Softcover, $12.95

Internal Growth Through Tao - New Publication!
Material goods can be passed from one person to another, but growth and awareness cannot be given in the same way. Spiritual development is related to one's own internal and external beingness. Through books, discussion or classes, wise people are able to use others' experiences to kindle their own inner light to help their own growth and live a life of no separation from their own spiritual nature. In this book, Master Ni teaches the more subtle, much deeper sphere of the reality of life that is above the shallow sphere of external achievement. He also shows the confusion caused by some spiritual teachings and guides you in the direction of developing spiritually by growing internally. 208 pages. Stock No. BINTE Softcover, $13.95

Power of Natural Healing - New Publication!
Master Ni discusses the natural capability of self-healing in this book, which is healing physical trouble untreated by medication or external measure. He offers information and practices which can assist any treatment method currently being used by someone seeking health. He goes deeper to discuss methods of Taoist cultivation which promote a healthy life, including Taoist spiritual achievement, which brings about health and longevity. This book is not only suitable for a person seeking to improve one's health condition. Those who wish to live long and happy, and to understand more about living a natural healthy lifestyle, may be supported by the practice of Taoist energy cultivation. 230 pages. Stock No. BPOWE Softcover, $14.95

Essence of Universal Spirituality

In this volume, as an open-minded learner and achieved teacher of universal spirituality, Master Ni examines and discusses all levels and topics of religious and spiritual teaching to help you develop your own correct knowledge of the essence existing above the differences in religious practice. He reviews religious teachings with hope to benefit modern people. This book is to help readers to come to understand the ultimate truth and enjoy the achievement of all religions without becoming confused by them. 304 pages. Stock No. BESSE Softcover, $19.95

Guide to Inner Light

Modern life is controlled by city environments, cultural customs, religious teachings and politics that can all divert our attention away from our natural life being. As a result, we lose the perspective of viewing ourselves as natural completeness. This book reveals the development of ancient Taoist adepts. Drawing inspiration from their experience, modern people looking for the true source and meaning of life can find great teachings to direct and benefit them. The invaluable ancient Taoist development can teach us to reach the attainable spiritual truth and point the way to the Inner Light. Master Ni uses the ancient high accomplishments to make this book a useful resource. 192 pages. Stock No. BGUID. Softcover, $12.95

Stepping Stones for Spiritual Success

In Asia, the custom of foot binding was followed for almost a thousand years. In the West, people did not bind feet, but they bound their thoughts for a much longer period, some 1,500 to 1,700 years. Their mind and thinking became unnatural. Being unnatural expresses a state of confusion where people do not know what is right. Once they become natural again, they are clear and progress is great. Master Ni invites his readers to unbind their minds; in this volume, he has taken the best of the traditional teachings and put them into contemporary language to make them more relevant to our time, culture and lives. 160 pages. Stock No. BSTEP. Softcover, $12.95.

The Complete Works of Lao Tzu

Lao Tzu's Tao Teh Ching is one of the most widely translated and cherished works of literature in the world. It presents the core of Taoist philosophy. Lao Tzu's timeless wisdom provides a bridge to subtle spiritual truth and practical guidelines for harmonious and peaceful living. Master Ni includes what is believed to be the only English translation of the Hua Hu Ching, a later work of Lao Tzu which has been lost to the general public for a thousand years. 212 pages. Stock No. BCOMP. Softcover, $12.95

Order The Complete Works of Lao Tzu and the companion Tao Teh Ching Cassette Tapes for only $25.00. Stock No. ABTAO.

The Book of Changes and the Unchanging Truth

The first edition of this book was widely appreciated by its readers, who drew great spiritual benefit from it. They found the principles of the I Ching to be clearly explained and useful to their lives, especially the commentaries. The legendary classic I Ching is recognized as mankind's first written book of wisdom. Leaders and sages throughout history have consulted it as a trusted advisor to reveal appropriate action to be taken in any of life's circumstances. This volume also includes over 200 pages of of material on Taoist principles of natural energy cycles, instruction and commentaries. New, revised second edition, 669 pages. Stock No. BBOOK. Hardcover, $35.95

The Story of Two Kingdoms
This volume is the metaphoric tale of the conflict between the Kingdoms of Light and Darkness. Through this unique story, Master Ni transmits the esoteric teachings of Taoism which have been carefully guarded secrets for over 5,000 years. This book is for those who are serious in their search and have devoted their lives to achieving high spiritual goals. 122 pages. Stock No. BSTOR. Hardcover, $14.95

The Way of Integral Life
This book can help build a bridge for those wishing to connect spiritual and intellectual development. It is most helpful for modern educated people. It includes practical and applicable suggestions for daily life, philosophical thought, esoteric insight and guidelines for those aspiring to give help and service to the world. This book helps you learn the wisdom of the ancient sages' achievement to assist the growth of your own wisdom and integrate it as your own new light and principles for balanced, reasonable living in worldly life. 320 pages. Softcover, $14.95, Stock No. BWAYS. Hardcover, $20.95, Stock No. BWAYH

Enlightenment: Mother of Spiritual Independence
The inspiring story and teachings of Master Hui Neng, the father of Zen Buddhism and Sixth Patriarch of the Buddhist tradition, highlight this volume. Hui Neng was a person of ordinary birth, intellectually unsophisticated, who achieved himself to become a spiritual leader. Master Ni includes enlivening commentaries and explanations of the principles outlined by this spiritual revolutionary. Having received the same training as all Zen Masters as one aspect of his training and spiritual achievement, Master Ni offers this teaching to guide his readers in their process of spiritual development. 264 pages. Softcover, $12.95, Stock No. BENLS. Hardcover, $18.95, Stock No. BENLH

Attaining Unlimited Life
The thought-provoking teachings of Chuang Tzu are presented in this volume. He was perhaps the greatest philosopher and master of Taoism and he laid the foundation for the Taoist school of thought. Without his work, people of later generations would hardly recognize the value of Lao Tzu's teaching in practical, everyday life. He touches the organic nature of human life more deeply and directly than that of other great teachers. This volume also includes questions by students and answers by Master Ni. 467 pages. Softcover, $18.95, Stock No. BATTS; Hardcover, $25.95, Stock No. BATTH

The Gentle Path of Spiritual Progress
This book offers a glimpse into the dialogues of a Taoist master and his students. In a relaxed, open manner, Master Ni, Hua-Ching explains to his students the fundamental practices that are the keys to experiencing enlightenment in everyday life. Many of the traditional secrets of Taoist training are revealed. His students also ask a surprising range of questions, and Master Ni's answers touch on contemporary psychology, finances, sexual advice, how to use the I Ching as well as the telling of some fascinating Taoist legends. Softcover, $12.95, Stock No. BGENT

Spiritual Messages from a Buffalo Rider, A Man of Tao
This is another important collection of Master Ni's service in his worldly trip, originally published as one half of The Gentle Path. He had the opportunity to meet people and answer their questions to help them gain the spiritual awareness that we live at the command of our animal nature. Our buffalo nature rides on us, whereas an achieved person rides the buffalo. In this book, Master Ni gives much helpful knowledge to those who are interested in improving their lives and deepening their cultivation so they too can develop beyond their mundane beings. Softcover, $12.95, Stock No. BSPIR

8,000 Years of Wisdom, Volume I and II
This two volume set contains a wealth of practical, down-to-earth advice given by Master Ni to his students over a five year period, 1979 to 1983. Drawing on his training in Traditional Chinese Medicine, Herbology, Acupuncture and other Taoist arts, Master Ni gives candid answers to students' questions on many topics ranging from dietary guidance to sex and pregnancy, meditation techniques and natural cures for common illnesses. Volume I includes dietary guidance; 236 pages; Stock No. BWIS1 Volume II includes sex and pregnancy guidance; 241 pages; Stock No. BWIS2. Softcover, Each Volume $12.95

The Uncharted Voyage Towards the Subtle Light
Spiritual life in the world today has become a confusing mixture of dying traditions and radical novelties. People who earnestly and sincerely seek something more than just a way to fit into the complexities of a modern structure that does not support true self-development often find themselves spiritually struggling. This book provides a profound understanding and insight into the underlying heart of all paths of spiritual growth, the subtle origin and the eternal truth of one universal life. 424 pages. Stock No. BUNCH. Softcover, $14.95

The Heavenly Way
A translation of the classic Tai Shan Kan Yin Pien (Straighten Your Way) and Yin Chia Wen (The Silent Way of Blessing). The treaties in this booklet are the main guidance for a mature and healthy life. The purpose of this booklet is to promote the recognition of truth, because only truth can teach the perpetual Heavenly Way by which one reconnects oneself with the divine nature. 41 pages. Stock No. BHEAV. Softcover, $2.95

Footsteps of the Mystical Child

This book poses and answers such questions as: What is a soul? What is wisdom? What is spiritual evolution? The answers to these and many other questions enable readers to open themselves to new realms of understanding and personal growth. There are also many true examples about people's internal and external struggles on the path of self-development and spiritual evolution. 166 pages. Stock No. BFOOT. Softcover, $9.95

Workbook for Spiritual Development

This book offers a practical, down-to-earth, hands-on approach for those who are devoted to the path of spiritual achievement. The reader will find diagrams showing fundamental hand positions to increase and channel one's spiritual energy, postures for sitting, standing and sleeping cultivation as well as postures for many Taoist invocations. The material in this workbook is drawn from the traditional teachings of Taoism and summarizes thousands of years of little known practices for spiritual development. An entire section is devoted to ancient invocations, another on natural celibacy and another on postures. In addition, Master Ni explains the basic attitudes and understandings that are the foundation for Taoist practices. 224 pages. Stock No. BWORK. Softcover, $12.95

Poster of Master Lu

Color poster of Master Lu, Tung Ping (shown on cover of workbook), for use with the workbook or in one's shrine. 16" x 22"; Stock No. PMLTP. $10.95

The Taoist Inner View of the Universe

This presentation of Taoist metaphysics provides guidance for one's own personal life transformation. Master Ni has given all the opportunity to know the vast achievement of the ancient unspoiled mind and its transpiercing vision. This book offers a glimpse of the inner world and immortal realm known to achieved Taoists and makes it understandable for students aspiring to a more complete life. 218 pages. Stock No. BTAOI. Softcover, $12.95

Tao, the Subtle Universal Law

Most people are unaware that their thoughts and behavior evoke responses from the invisible net of universal energy. The real meaning of Taoist self-discipline is to harmonize with universal law. To lead a good stable life is to be aware of the actual conjoining of the universal subtle law with every moment of our lives. This book presents the wisdom and practical methods that the ancient Chinese have successfully used for centuries to accomplish this. 165 pages. Stock No. TAOS. Softcover, $7.95

MATERIALS ON TAOIST HEALTH, ARTS AND SCIENCES

BOOKS

The Tao of Nutrition by Maoshing Ni, Ph.D., with Cathy McNease, B.S., M.H. - Working from ancient Chinese medical classics and contemporary research, Dr. Maoshing Ni and Cathy McNease have compiled an indispensable guide to natural healing. This exceptional book shows the reader how to take control of one's health through one's eating habits. This volume contains 3 major sections: the first section deals with theories of Chinese nutrition and philosophy; the second describes over 100 common foods in detail, listing their energetic properties, therapeutic actions and individual remedies. The third section lists nutritional remedies for many common ailments. This book presents both a healing system and a disease prevention system which is flexible in adapting to every individual's needs. 214 pages. Stock No. BNUTR. Softcover, $14.95

Chinese Vegetarian Delights by Lily Chuang
An extraordinary collection of recipes based on principles of traditional Chinese nutrition. Many recipes are therapeutically prepared with herbs. Diet has long been recognized as a key factor in health and longevity. For those who require restricted diets and those who choose an optimal diet, this cookbook is a rare treasure. Meat, sugar, diary products and fried foods are excluded. Produce, grains, tofu, eggs and seaweeds are imaginatively prepared. 104 pages. Stock No. BCHIV. Softcover, $7.95

Chinese Herbology Made Easy - by Maoshing Ni, Ph.D.
This text provides an overview of Oriental medical theory, in-depth descriptions of each herb category, with over 300 black and white photographs, extensive tables of individual herbs for easy reference, and an index of pharmaceutical and Pin-Yin names. The distillation of over-whelming material into essential elements enables one to focus efficiently and develop a clear understanding of Chinese herbology. This book is especially helpful for those studying for their California Acupuncture License. 202 pages. Stock No. BCHIH. Softcover, 14.95

Crane Style Chi Gong Book - By Daoshing Ni, Ph.D.
Chi Gong is a set of meditative exercises that was developed several thousand years ago by Taoists in China. It is now practiced for healing purposes, combining breathing techniques, body movements and mental imagery to guide the smooth flow of energy throughout the body. This book gives a more detailed account and study of Chi Gong than the videotape alone. It may be used with or without the videotape. Includes complete instructions and information on using Chi Gong exercise as a medical therapy. 55 pages. Stock No. BCRAN. Spiral bound $10.95

VIDEO TAPES

Physical Movement for Spiritual Learning: Dao-In Physical Art for a Long and Happy Life (VHS) - by Master Ni.
Dao-In is a series of typical Taoist movements which are traditionally used for physical energy conducting. These exercises were passed down from the ancient achieved Taoists and immortals. The ancients discovered that Dao-In exercises not only solved problems of stagnant energy, but also increased their health and lengthened their years. The exercises are also used as practical support for cultivation and the higher achievements of spiritual immortality. Master Ni, Hua-Ching, heir to the tradition of the achieved masters, is the first one who releases this important Taoist practice to the modern world in this 1 hour videotape. VHS $59.95

T'ai Chi Chuan: An Appreciation (VHS) - by Master Ni
Different styles of T'ai Chi Ch'uan as Movement have different purposes and accomplish different results. In this long awaited videotape, Master Ni, Hua-Ching presents three styles of T'ai Chi Movement handed down to him through generations of highly developed masters. They are the "Gentle Path," "Sky Journey," and "Infinite Expansion" styles of T'ai Chi Movement. The three styles are presented uninterrupted in this unique videotape and are set to music for observation and appreciation. VHS 30 minutes $49.95

Crane Style Chi Gong (VHS) - by Dr. Daoshing Ni, Ph.D.
Chi Gong is a set of meditative exercises developed several thousand years ago by ancient Taoists in China. It is now practiced for healing stubborn chronic diseases, strengthening the body to prevent disease and as a tool for further spiritual enlightenment. It combines breathing techniques, simple body movements, and mental imagery to guide the smooth flow of energy throughout the body. Chi gong is easy to learn for all ages. Correct and persistent practice will increase one's energy, relieve stress or tension, improve concentration and clarity, release emotional stress and restore general well-being. 2 hours Stock No. VCRAN. $65.95

Eight Treasures (VHS) - By Maoshing Ni, Ph.D.
These exercises help open blocks in a person's energy flow and strengthen one's vitality. It is a complete exercise combining physical stretching and toning and energy conducting movements coordinated with breathing. The Eight Treasures are an exercise unique to the Ni family. Patterned from nature, the 32 movements of the Eight Treasures are an excellent foundation for Tai Chi Chuan or martial arts. 1 hour and 45 minutes. Stock No. VEIGH. $49.95

Tai Chi Chuan I & II (VHS) - By Maoshing Ni, Ph.D.
This exercise integrates the flow of physical movement with that of integral energy in the Taoist style of "Harmony," similar to the long form of Yang-style Tai Chi Chuan. Tai Chi has been practiced for thousands of years to help both physical longevity and spiritual cultivation. 1 hour each. Each Video Tape $49.95. Order both for $90.00. Stock Nos: Part I, VTAI1; Part II, VTAI2; Set of two, VTAI3.

AUDIO CASSETTES

Invocations: Health and Longevity and Healing a Broken Heart - By Maoshing Ni, Ph.D.
This audio cassette guides the listener through a series of ancient invocations to channel and conduct one's own healing energy and vital force. "Thinking is louder than thunder." The mystical power by which all miracles are brought about is your sincere practice of this principle. 30 minutes. Stock No. AINVO. $5.95

Chi Gong for Stress Release - By Maoshing Ni, Ph.D.
This audio cassette guides you through simple, ancient breathing exercises that enable you to release day-to-day stress and tension that are such a common cause of illness today. 30 minutes. Stock No. ACHIS. $8.95

Chi Gong for Pain Management - By Maoshing Ni, Ph.D.
Using easy visualization and deep-breathing techniques that have been developed over thousands of years, this audio cassette offers methods for overcoming pain by invigorating your energy flow and unblocking obstructions that cause pain. 30 minutes. Stock No. ACHIP. $8.95

Tao Teh Ching Cassette Tapes
This classic work of Lao Tzu has been recorded in this two-cassette set that is a companion to the book translated by Master Ni. Professionally recorded and read by Robert Rudelson. 120 minutes. Stock No. ATAOT. $15.95

Order Master Ni's book, The Complete Works of Lao Tzu, and Tao Teh Ching Cassette Tapes for only $25.00. Stock No. ABTAO.

Many people write or call asking for information on how to set up study groups or centers in their own community. To respond to such requests, the Center for Taoist Arts in Atlanta, Georgia has offered to show others how they have set up their own center and discussion group. If you are interested, please contact Frank Gibson, The Center for Taoist Arts, PO Box 1389, Alpharetta, GA 30239-1389.

How To Order

Complete this form and mail it to: **Union of Tao and Man,**
117 Stonehaven Way, Los Angeles, CA 90049 (213)-472-9970

Name: _____

Address: _____

City: _____ State: _____ Zip: _____

Phone - Daytime: _____ Evening: _____

(We may telephone you if we have questions about your order.)

Qty.	Stock No.	Title/Description	Price Each	Total Price

Total amount for items ordered _____

Sales tax (CA residents, 6-1/2%) _____

Shipping Charge (See below) _____

Total Amount Enclosed _____

Please allow 6 - 8 weeks for delivery.
Thank you for your order.

U. S. Funds Only, Please
Please write your check or money order
to Union of Tao and Man

Shipping Charge - All Orders Sent Via U.S. Postal Service, unless specified.
Domestic Surface Mail: First item $2.00, each additional, add $.50.
Canada/Mexico Surface Mail: First item $2.50, each additional, add $1.00.
Other Foreign Surface Mail: First Item $3.00, each additional, add $2.00.
Foreign Air Mail: First item $18.00, each additional, add $7.00.

Credit Card orders only:

VISA **MasterCard**

☐ Visa (13 or 16 digits)   ☐ MasterCard (16 digits)

Card Account Number

| 1 | 2 | 3 | 4 | 5 | 6 | 7 | 8 | 9 | 10 | 11 | 12 | 13 | 14 | 15 | 16 |

Expiration Date ☐☐ — ☐☐

Signature: _____

Spiritual Study Through the College of Tao

The College of Tao and the Union of Tao and Man were established formally in California in the 1970's. This tradition is a very old spiritual culture of mankind, holding long experience of human spiritual growth. Its central goal is to offer healthy spiritual education to all people of our society. This time tested tradition values the spiritual development of each individual self and passes down its guidance and experience.

Master Ni carries his tradition from its country of origin to the west. He chooses to avoid making the mistake of old-style religions that have rigid establishments which resulted in fossilizing the delicacy of spiritual reality. Rather, he prefers to guide the teachings of his tradition as a school of no boundary rather than a religion with rigidity. Thus, the branches or centers of this Taoist school offer different programs of similar purpose. Each center extends its independent service, but all are unified in adopting Master Ni's work as the foundation of teaching to fulfill the mission of providing spiritual education to all people.

The centers offer their classes, teaching, guidance and practices on building the groundwork for cultivating a spiritually centered and well-balanced life. As a person obtains the correct knowledge with which to properly guide himself or herself, he or she can then become more skillful in handling the experiences of daily life. The assimilation of good guidance in one's practical life brings about different stages of spiritual development.

Any interested individual is welcome to join and learn to grow for oneself. You might like to join the center near where you live, or you yourself may be interested in organizing a center or study group based on the model of existing centers. In that way, we all work together for the spiritual benefit of all people. We do not require any religious type of commitment.

The learning is life. The development is yours. The connection of study may be helpful, useful and serviceable, directly to you.

- -

Mail to: Union of Tao and Man, 117 Stonehaven Way, Los Angeles, CA 90049

_____ I wish to be put on the mailing list of the Union of Tao and Man to be notified of classes, educational activities and new publications.

Name:_____

Address:_____

City:_____State:_____Zip:_____

Herbs Used by Ancient Taoist Masters

The pursuit of everlasting youth or immortality throughout human history is an innate human desire. Long ago, Chinese esoteric Taoists went to the high mountains to contemplated nature, strengthen their bodies, empower their minds and develop their spirit. From their studies and cultivation, they gave China alchemy and chemistry, herbology and acupuncture, the I Ching, astrology, martial arts and T'ai Chi Chuan, Chi Gong and many other useful kinds of knowledge.

Most important, they handed down in secrecy methods for attaining longevity and spiritual immortality. There were different levels of approach; one was to use a collection of food herb formulas that were only available to highly achieved Taoist masters. They used these food herbs to increase energy and heighten vitality. This treasured collection of herbal formulas remained within the Ni family for centuries.

Now, through Traditions of Tao, the Ni family makes these foods available for you to use to assist the foundation of your own positive development. It is only with a strong foundation that expected results are produced from diligent cultivation.

As a further benefit, in concert with the Taoist principle of self-sufficiency, Traditions of Tao offers the food herbs along with the Union of Tao and Man's publications in a distribution opportunity for anyone serious about financial independence.

Send to: *Traditions of Tao*
                   c/o 117 Stonehaven Way
                   Los Angeles, CA 90049

❑ *Please send me a Traditions of Tao brochure.*

❑ *Please send me information on becoming an independent distributor of Traditions of Tao herbal products and publications.*

Name _____

*Address*_____

*City*_____*State*_____*Zip*_____

*Phone (day)*_____*(night)*_____

Yo San University of Traditional Chinese Medicine
"Not just a medical career, but a life-time commitment to raising one's spiritual standard."

Thank you for your support and interest in our publications and services. It is by your patronage that we continue to offer you the practical knowledge and wisdom from this venerable Taoist tradition.

Because of your sustained interest in Taoism, we formed Yo San University of Traditional Chinese Medicine, a non-profit educational institute in January 1989 under the direction of founder Master Ni, Hua-Ching. Yo San University is the continuation of 38 generations of Ni family practitioners who handed down knowledge and wisdom from fathers to sons. Its purpose is to train and graduate practitioners of the highest caliber in Traditional Chinese Medicine, which includes acupuncture, herbology and spiritual development.

We view Traditional Chinese Medicine as the application of spiritual development. Its foundation is the spiritual capability to know life, to know a person's problem and how to cure it. We teach students how to care for themselves and others, and emphasize the integration of traditional knowledge and modern science. We offer a complete Master's degree program approved by the California State Department of Education that provides an excellent education in Traditional Chinese Medicine and meets all requirements for state licensure.

We invite you to inquire into our school about a creative and rewarding career as a holistic physician. Classes are also open to persons interested only in self-enrichment. For more information, please fill out the form below and send it to:

Yo San University,
12304 Santa Monica Blvd. Suite 104,
Los Angeles, CA 90025

❑ Please send me information on the Masters degree program in Traditional Chinese Medicine.

❑ Please send me information on health workshops and seminars.

❑ Please send me information on continuing education for acupuncturists and health professionals.

Name _____

Address_____

City_____State_____Zip_____

Phone(day)_____(night)_____